DOUGLAS KAINE MCKELVEY

EVERY
moment
HOLY

VOLUME I
POCKET EDITION

EVERY MOMENT HOLY:
VOLUME ONE POCKET EDITION
©2019 Douglas McKelvey

Rabbit Room Press | 3321 Stephens Hill Lane,
Nashville, TN 37013 | info@rabbitroom.com

TEXT Douglas McKelvey
ART/DESIGN Ned Bustard
EDITING Pete Peterson

ISBN 9781951872021

Printed in China

For those
who went before,
for those
who walk beside,
and for those
who will
follow after.

SO WE, THOUGH MANY,
ARE ONE BODY IN CHRIST,
AND INDIVIDUALLY MEMBERS
ONE OF ANOTHER.
—ROMANS 12:5

THEREFORE ENCOURAGE
ONE ANOTHER AND
BUILD ONE ANOTHER UP,
JUST AS YOU ARE DOING.
—1 THESSALONIANS 5:11

IF YOU'D LIKE TO PRINT COPIES OF A LITURGY FROM THIS BOOK
FOR USE AT A FAMILY GATHERING OR PUBLIC EVENT, INDIVIDUAL
LITURGIES ARE AVAILABLE FOR DOWNLOAD AT
WWW.EVERYMOMENTHOLY.COM.

VISIT THE WEBSITE FOR MORE INFORMATION.

CONTENTS

CONTENTS

LITURGIES OF CREATION & RECREATION

CONTENTS

CONTENTS

CONTENTS

NOTES ON USING THIS BOOK

IN THE FOLLOWING PAGES you will find liturgies for use in a number of different ways. Some are meant to be read by a "Leader" and the "People," as in a traditional liturgical service or responsive reading. Others are intended for personal use, either read silently or aloud. And still others may contain multiple speaking parts for use in a group (such as the members of a wedding party).

However, none of these formats should be considered rigid. One might choose to split up a personal liturgy to be read in parts by a group for whom the subject is applicable. And likewise, those liturgies written for a "Leader" and "People" may be of equal value to the lone reader.

Some prayers are written with the intent of daily or routine recitation, and others are for use on special, memorable, difficult, or even tragic occasions. The prayers included in the "Litugies of the Moment" section are designed for memorization so that they can be recalled at need.

Formally, the book is divided into sections, but the prayers themselves are often difficult to assign to specific categories. As such, the categories themselves should be considered guidelines. For instance, "A Liturgy Before Consuming Media" appears under "Liturgies of Creation and Recreation," but could have been under "Liturgies of Petition and Provision."

FOREWORD

BY ANDREW PETERSON

WENDELL BERRY WROTE, "There are no unsacred places; there are only sacred places and desecrated places." In that spirit, this book reminds us that there are no unsacred moments; there are only sacred moments and moments we have forgotten are sacred. If that's true, then it is our duty to reclaim the sacredness of our lives, of life itself. And the first step is to remember—to remember the dream of Eden that shimmers at the edges of things, to remember that the madman on the corner was made in God's image, to remember that work and play and suffering and celebration are all sentences in a good story being told by God, a story arcing its way to a new creation. By remembering the holiness of each moment we banish that old Gnostic ghost and thwart its lie that there's nothing holy about flesh and bone, soil and stone, work and pleasure and all tangible, tactile, visible things. The resurrection of Jesus sent shockwaves into every molecule of creation, even into this crazy century of ones and zeroes and jet engines. If the Gospel is true, then it matters in all of time and space—from a thousand years ago at the Norman conquest of England to ten minutes ago when I ate a cookie; it matters from the moons of Jupiter to the couch where I'm writing this. Yes, I realize that I just conjured the less-than-flattering image of myself lazing on a couch, brushing cookie crumbs from my laptop—but that's exactly the point. The Gospel matters even here. Even now.

We at Rabbit Room Press give you *Every Moment Holy* in the hope that it will become a book you'll find yourself reaching for again and again. Douglas McKelvey is one of the finest writers of our time. He's labored long over every word in this book, bringing his love for Jesus, his poetry, and his storytelling to bear on a work that has already blessed our family. When we've feasted with friends, when our family dog died, when we arrived at the Atlantic for holiday, when we sat on the hill over our home to watch the sunset, when I planted flowers in the garden, when my sons and I watched a series on Netflix, we read aloud Doug's liturgies to remind ourselves of the sacredness of all things, of the pervasive truth of the Gospel. Maybe you're new to liturgy, maybe it has long been part of your tradition—either way, our hope is that you would let these prayers edify you, reshape your thinking, recalibrate your compass, ignite your imagination, and pique your longing for the world to come. Doug's robust theology has come together with artist Ned Bustard's profoundly meaningful artwork (every inch of every illustration is crammed with Christian imagery) to create a book that we hope will live on for generations to come, giving voice to prayers we didn't know we needed to pray, as the kingdom comes on earth—in every holy moment—just as it is in heaven.

A LITURGY FOR THE
Writing of Liturgies

How fearful a vocation is the writing of liturgies,
O Lord, for it presumes the shaping
of words that others will speak to You.

Therefore make me faithful to my craft,
    O Great Architect of Truth & Poetry.
Let me be diligent to the discipline and
the labor required, but let me never
forget that all such measured faithfulness
yields only a polished stone, meaningless
until it is stirred from within by your breath,
until it is set by you in a crown of your own crafting.

Grant to me then, an unmerited wisdom
to anticipate the needs of your people
in their varied seasons of life. Let me find form
to convey their loves and fears, their thoughts
and hopes, their sorrows and their celebrations.
Inspire me to tell in words, of the holiness of your presence
made manifest in all tasks, at all hours of all days.
    For you, O Lord, are with us always.

Every sphere of life and creation is Yours,
and all are threads of the same bright weave:
    our goings-out and our comings-in,
    our fellowship and our loneliness,
    our youth and our old age,
    our passions and our vocations,
    our chores and our entertainments.

You are equally present in our failures and
in our successes,
    in our sleep and in our wakeful hours,
    in our tears and in our laughter,
    in our births, in our lives,
and even in the hours of our deaths.
You are everpresent with us.

May this book and these prayers therefore
    serve to train the hearts of your people
to practice a mindfulness of your presence
    in all moments.

Move within these liturgies, O Spirit of God!
    Stir these pages. Stir hearts. Stir minds.
    Stir imaginations.

Call your peoples to remember you always.
O peoples of God! Remember your God!
　　Remember him in all places.
　　Remember him at all times.
　　Remember his grace and his love.
　　Remember his comfort and his mercy.
　　Remember his beauty and his wonder.
　　Remember his instruction and his holiness.
He is here. He is with you every moment.

Every moment is holy.

Amen.

LITURGIES OF
The Hours

A LITURGY OF
The Hours: *Daybreak*

THE LEADER SHOULD CHOOSE A SHORT PASSAGE OF
SCRIPTURE FOR THE DAY'S CONTEMPLATION BEFORE BEGINNING.
THIS SAME PASSAGE WILL BE READ DURING EACH
"LITURGY OF THE HOURS" THIS DAY.

LEADER: O children of the Living God,
what is your Father's greatest desire
for you this day?
PEOPLE: **That we should love our eternal King**
with all our hearts,
with all our souls,
with all our minds
and with all our strength.

And how would you show this love?
By remembering him at all times.
By cultivating thankfulness
for his many blessings, and trusting
his good providence
for the meeting of our needs.
By loving all whose lives intersect our own.
By choosing to serve rather

than to be served, to be wounded
rather than to wound, and by bearing
patiently with the failings of others,
extending the same kindness,
mercy, and compassion that God in Christ
has so graciously offered us.

We would also love him by serving
with faithfulness and due passion
in our various vocations,
by delighting in all things he has created
for our benefit and pleasure, and by caring well
    for all he has given us to steward.
O children of the Living God, you would do well
    to practice your love in these ways today!

Do you now possess the needed strength
to perfectly accomplish such holy requirements?
We do not. We are weak and inconsistent,
and often buffeted by fear and pride
and selfishness. But being impoverished
and ill-equipped as we are,
we will look to the grace of God
and to the sanctifying work of the Spirit
to accomplish his purposes
in and through us this day,

as we, in grateful response,
seek to choose that which pleases him.
We open our hearts anew to you this morning,
O Lord, that the love of the Father
> and the life of Christ
> and the breath of the Spirit
would quicken within us
a greater affection for your ways.
Work your will in us, Lord Christ.

Let us now bring before our gracious God
any petitions relevant to this day.
O Lord, hear our prayers.

PARTICIPANTS MAY NOW OFFER SPECIFIC PRAYERS,
EITHER SILENTLY OR ALOUD.

O children of God, casting your cares
upon his strong shoulders,
now surrender your own agendas for this day,
> and instead be led by the workings of his Spirit.
Open our eyes and our hearts, O Lord,
to your words and truth.

May these words of God bring to each of us
conviction, challenge, and comfort,
as our lives and choices this day require.
Shape us even now, O Lord.

Prepare our bodies for the labors of this day.
**Give us strength and health
to complete them.**
Prepare our minds for the demands of this day.
Grant us clarity, creativity, and discernment.
Prepare our souls for those sorrows and joys
and celebrations and disappointments
we will encounter, that every circumstance
would serve only to draw us nearer to you.
**May our words, our choices,
and our actions today be offered
as true expressions of worship.**
Now you who are loved of God,
step forward into this new day
appointed by him, that you might

journey through its hours
in the peace and the grace
and the love of your Lord.
Lead us this day, Lord Christ,
that we might walk its paths
in the light of the hope of our
coming redemption.

Amen.

A LITURGY OF
The Hours: *Midday*

LEADER: O Christ our rest,
We pause amidst the labors of this day
to remember the best reason for our laboring.
PEOPLE: **We labor, O Lord, as stewards of**
your creation, and as stewards of the gifts
you have apportioned to each of us
for the good of all.
Bless then the works of our hands
and minds and hearts, O God,
    that they might bear fruit for your greater purposes.

May our work this day be rendered
first as service to you, that the benefits
>   **of it might be eternal.**
Receive this, the offering of our labors, O Lord.
Amen.

If our hearts have already been tempted this day
to believe anything about ourselves or others
that does not take into account your creation,
>   your mercy, your sacrifice, your grace,
>   your forgiveness, your redemption,
>   and your unshakeable love, O God,
remind us again of these truths,
giving us faith enough to believe
and hope enough to choose
to embrace them again and again.

Or if we have been swayed from the place of
resting in your grace today—swayed by shame,
by error, by vanity, by pride, or by love of the
praise of people, act, O Holy Spirit!
Reveal our error, convict conscience,
and bring us to quick repentance.
Rekindle our affections, restoring them again
to their one worthy object, who is Christ,
and who alone holds the words of eternal life.

Let us now consider such words.
Shape our thoughts O Lord, by your truth,
even as you shape our hearts by your love.

THE SHORT PASSAGE OF SCRIPTURE CHOSEN FOR
THE DAY'S CONTEMPLATION IS HERE READ ALOUD
BY ONE OF THE PARTICIPANTS. A MOMENT OF SILENCE
IS THEN TAKEN FOR REFLECTION.

Now grant us strength and grace, O God,
sufficient to the remains of the day,
that we might move through its unfolding
in humble obedience to your will
and in sensitivity to your Spirit
and in joyful expectancy of your coming kingdom.
May the light of that eternal city
illuminate our hearts, our paths, our vision
through these next hours, O Lord.

Amen.

A LITURGY OF
The Hours: *Nightfall*

LEADER: Here at day's end we seek you,
O King of Earth and Heaven.
PEOPLE: **You have been our sustenance**
across the sunlit hours.
Be now our counselor, comforter, and
protector in dark of night.
Amen.

We now give thanks to God for
the blessings of the day that has passed.
We praise you, O Father, for the provision
of food, and shelter, and fellowship,
and for all other evidences of grace
that have been ours. May our hearts
always receive such gifts from your hand,
with true humility and thankfulness.
Amen.

Now let us ready our hearts to make confession
for the imperfections of our love this day.

A MOMENT OF REFLECTIVE SILENCE IS KEPT.

Holy Spirit, grant us each a true conviction
    leading to a true repentance.
**Indeed it was our desire to serve you well
in this day, O God, but we have again fallen
short of your righteousness in our thoughts,
our intentions, our actions, and our
utterances. We have responded at times
without grace. We have chosen sometimes
that which is unprofitable and which leads
neither to our own flourishing nor to the
proclamation of your glory. Forgive us,
O King, for treasons both known and
unknown. Forgive us for the harms
we have done this day, and for the goods
we might have done but failed to do;
forgive us also for the constant condition
of our hearts, for the self-serving impulses,
inclinations, and desires which stand us
every moment in need of a savior.**
How graciously he receives your repentances!

God be merciful to we who are sinners!
Take joy, all you who are called by his name,
for his mercies are already yours!
Thanks be to God!

Now may the grace of his forgiveness,
which blooms evergreen for all his children,
work powerfully in us, changing us into
better image-bearers of Christ and
more faithful servants of our king.
Let our inability to ever perfectly love you,
O God, drive us daily to the arms of Christ,
wherein the enormity of your mercy and
the scandal of such grace lavished upon us
would birth in us a new and greater
affection for you, and a new and greater
desire to do that which pleases you.
Somehow use even our weaknesses for your glory.

Now hear these words of favor,
O children of God: All these sins you have truly repented of,
he has eternally forgiven. They will never be held against you.
You are free to love and to serve him in joyful assurance,
knowing his grace will always be more
than sufficient to your own failings.
Thanks be to Christ for this glorious gift!
Amen.

Resting now, O Lord, in the certain promise of your love—
through which we are adopted as your daughters and sons—
we find ourselves at ease in your holy presence,
bringing to you our diverse burdens and petitions this night.
Heavenly Father, hear our prayers.

PARTICIPANTS MAY NOW OFFER SPECIFIC PRAYERS,
EITHER SILENTLY OR ALOUD.

Thank you, O Lord, that you are
attentive to the cries of your children.
Deepen now our knowledge of you,
and our love for your truth.
Tender our hearts to receive your words.

THE SHORT PASSAGE OF SCRIPTURE CHOSEN FOR
THE DAY'S CONTEMPLATION IS HERE READ ALOUD
BY ONE OF THE PARTICIPANTS. A MOMENT OF SILENCE
IS THEN TAKEN FOR REFLECTION.

Retire now, you children of God,
contemplating his words and resting
in the peace of the surety of the love
he has extended to you in Christ.
Know this night the comfort of his Spirit,
who ever abides in and among us,

drawing us always toward our
ultimate redemption at the renewing
of body and soul and of all creation.
**Praise be to God, for his mysteries
yet to be revealed.**

Indeed, an hour is coming
when we shall find ourselves
freed at last from the very presence of sin,
and liberated to live eternally in that
glorious freedom and knowledge
and beauty and perfection
which was ever our intended birthright.
**Even now, O Lord,
in the dark of this night,
let our lives be lit by rumors
of these coming glories.**

Amen.

LITURGIES OF
Labor
& Vocation

A LITURGY FOR
Domestic Days

Many are the things that must be daily done.
Meet me therefore, O Lord,
in the doing of the small, repetitive tasks,

In the cleaning and ordering and
maintenance and stewardship of things—
    of dishes, of floors, of carpets
    and toilets and tubs,
    of scrubbing and sweeping
    and dusting and laundering—
That by such stewardship I might bring
a greater order to my own life,
and to the lives of any I am given to serve,
so that in those ordered spaces bright things might flourish:
    fellowship and companionship,
    creativity and conversation,
    learning and laughter
    and enjoyment and health.

As I steward the small, daily tasks, may I remember
    these good ends, and so discover in my labors
    the promise of the eternal hopes that underlie them.

High King of Heaven,
you showed yourself among us as the servant of all,
speaking stories of a kingdom to come, a kingdom in which
those who spend themselves for love, even in the humblest of
services, will not be forgotten, but whose every service lovingly
rendered will be seen from that far vantage as the planting
of a precious seed blooming into eternity.

And so I offer this small service to you, O Lord,
for you make no distinction between those acts
that bring a person the wide praise of their peers
and those unmarked acts that are accomplished
       in a quiet obedience without accolade.
You see instead the heart, the love, and the
       faithful stewardship of all labors, great and small.

And so, in your loving presence, I undertake this task.

O God, grant that my heart might be ordered aright,
knowing that all good service faithfully rendered
is first a service rendered unto you.
       Receive then this my service, that even in the midst
of labors that hold no happiness in themselves,
I might have increasing joy.

Amen.

A LITURGY FOR ONE
Who Is Employed

O Christ who supplies my every need,
I praise you for all provisions
    and for the means by which they are provided.
For my current employment,
    in this season of life, I give you thanks.
By it, may I meet my own needs,
    and contribute to the needs of others.

Let me work and serve in this position
with mindfulness, creativity, and kindness,
    loving you well by loving all
    whom I encounter here.

Jesus, be everpresent as mediator
    between me and my employer,
    between me and my supervisors and co-workers,
and in all my dealings with others in this work,
reminding me that my treatment of them
is the strongest evidence of my affection for you.

Grant me therefore the patience to listen to others,
the humility to learn from them, the compassion to consider

their needs as my own, and the grace to wear well in this place
the name of my Lord, remembering that I arrive here each day
as an emissary of your kingdom.

Let me be an asset to my employer and superiors,
      working for their flourishing without resentment.
Let me be a support to my peers,
      contributing to their advancement without jealousy.
Let me be an encouragement to any I train or lead,
      affirming and equipping them without disdain.

May the days of my employment here be meaningful.
Use this chapter in my life to accomplish your ends,
      whatever they might be.

May my presence here daily suggest your presence here.
And may the outworking of the gospel
be always evident in this my work,
that my service as an employee
might be ever reckoned and received
as service first rendered unto you, O Christ.

Amen.

A LITURGY FOR THOSE WHO
Employ Others

What a gift, O Lord, to be so blessed
that I might extend this bounty to others
in the form of honest employment,
whereby they might also bless and provide
for those who depend upon them.

Teach me each day the way of Christ—
how better to serve those I would lead.

Give me wisdom and mercy in my dealings with those I hire.
May I be patient, and gracious, and slow to anger,
recognizing always your image within those I employ.
May I trust first in you as my provision, that I might
relate to others not as tools and commodities, but as
fellow pilgrims and fellow beggars, desperate for divine love.

Teach me to seek the eternal good of my employees,
        even over my own profits.
Let me relate to each of these, your unique creations,
in light of the priorities, not of the kingdoms of this world,
but of the better kingdom of Heaven.

And may I, by the graciousness of my interactions with these
employees, establish a tone and a culture of kindness and grace
that will permeate every room and corridor and hall of this
building like a sweet perfume, like the aroma of Christ.

May those who labor here do so with
    a sense of peace
    and purpose
    and calm,
with a sense that they are valued and respected
and appreciated, and may my dealings with them be
a steady witness and invitation, beckoning each to respond
more fully to the call of your Spirit.

O Lord, be present in this place.
Be at work in our work.
Be at your labors in this place of our labor.

IF APPROPRIATE TO THE WORK SETTING, ADD:

Brood over the cubicles and the break rooms,
    the desks and departments,
    the offices and the factory floors.
Brood over this space and these people.
Brood brightly, and bring forth new joy, new hope, new life!

Amen.

A LITURGY FOR
Laundering

May I recall in this needful parable
    of soil and rags,
    of soap and water and cleansing,
the work which you have done for your people,
O Christ, and the work which you are now
doing, in me. Even as the waters are agitated
and churned, stir by your Holy Spirit
my heart and memory and conscience.

Open my eyes to see my own faults,
    my own weaknesses,
    the harms I have caused
    and the griefs I have inflicted—
Not so that I would sit in an impassable guilt,
    but so that I would be stirred
to fresh repentance, to the making of amends
where amends can be made, and to prayer
and trust that your Spirit might cleanse
those things which I have stained by my own
selfishness, bitterness, jealousy, pride,
or impatience.

Even as I draw the freshly laundered clothes
from the basin, may the sight and the scent
of a new cleanness remind me

> of the righteousness that is now mine,
> of the ongoing forgiveness that you extend,
> of your work on my behalf
>> which is both finished, and forever
>> ongoing and necessary in this life.

In Christ you have declared me righteous.
Yet by your Spirit I pray

> You would ever continue to cleanse me,
> sanctifying me that my aroma,
> day to day and week to week,

might be more and more like that of Christ.

A LITURGY FOR THE
Preparation of a Meal

LEADER: O Bread of Life,
PEOPLE: **Meet us in the making of this meal.**

As we perform the various tasks of washing, chopping, sifting,
mixing, simmering, baking, and boiling,

let those little acts coalesce
into an embodied liturgy of service—
an outworking of love offered for your purposes,
that through us, your tender care might be translated into
the comforting and cheery language of nurturing food
and drink offered for the benefit of others.

Let us invest in this preparation
a lovingkindness toward those who will partake.
Let us craft this meal with a care
as would befit any endeavor touching eternity.

Meet us in the making of this meal, O Lord,
and make of it something more
than a mere nourishment for the body.
Make it the center of a sheltered space where grace freely flows.
Let the slow savoring of these foods give pause
to those who will soon partake, prompting them
to linger long at table, taking rest from the labors of the day,
engaging in good conversation.

Let the comforting qualities of the dishes we prepare,
become catalysts for a rich fellowship, a warm consolation,
and a fruitful increase of holy affections.

May this meal serve to remind those who share its pleasures
of the goodness and the hope that infuses all creation.

Unto that end, let us labor creatively,
    with imaginations engaged,
knowing that we are cooks in the kitchen—yes—
but we are also agents of a deep eternity,
whose prepared meals might feed more than the body,
nourishing also the hearts and hopes of those
sometimes-weary souls who are well-served by our labors.

Amen.

A LITURGY FOR THE
Preparation of an Artisanal Meal

Is it possible that a meal might be so infused with
a holy artistry, so thoughtfully prepared with intent
to convey comfort and delight, as to make the one
who consumes it remember again, even for a moment,
that there is a God, and that his care for them is tender?

Then let us set about to make that meal, O Lord.

Let us ply our culinary craft as a poet
    might approach her masterwork,
weighing each word and phrasing with deliberate intention,
shaping the design as a whole,
        while working nuanced echoes of
        some major theme into the finer details.

Let us thoughtfully consider and carefully construct
the layered experience of those who will consume
what we create, so that its pleasures and surprises
will unfold sequentially to the eyes, the nose, the tongue,
        as a poem composed of taste and texture.

Let us labor with attention paid
    to the tinglings of heat and spice,
    to the interplay of herbs and oils,
        to the mingling of things sweet and tart, salty and sour.

Let us paint in pleasing combinations of colors
arrayed upon the plate, in complimentary arrangements
of line and form, in a medley of aromas
blending into one bouquet.

Let us play with a glad cascade of sumptuous and savory flavors.

Let us stretch our artistry, O Lord,
    using every means at our disposal,
to craft a meal that might awaken in the souls of those
who share it a yearning hunger which might
only be finally satisfied
    by the Bread of Life,
    and the Wine of God,
at the time of the world's remaking.

Let us make this day a meal that would point to that day,
a meal to remind of the beauty and the love
and the promise undergirding all creation.

Let us make a meal to remind our pilgrim guests
that life will not always be so burdened,
that their days of exile will end, and that they will feast at last
joyfully in the city of their hope, at the table of
their God-King, at the wedding feast of their Prince, at the
dawning of a golden age, untouched by mortal sorrows.

If such a meal can be made by these hands in this kitchen,
O Lord, then let us breathe here the breath of your Spirit,
and let us set about to make that meal.

Amen.

A LITURGY FOR THE
Hurried Preparation of a Meal

Lord, I have little time to build this meal,
but I would still make of it a holy offering.

Let me work into these rapid preparations
a care and a kindness for those who will partake.

Even in our common haste,
may this meal serve as a catalyst for a deeper grace,
    reminding us to be ever thankful.
Let those who share this food embrace the fellowship
of the moment,
    however fleeting,
and let them rise from the table knowing
that even in their comings and their goings,
    they are nurtured and loved.

Grant also, O Lord, that we, at other times in our busy lives,
might make ample margin for more unhurried meals,
and for a more leisurely fellowship.

Amen.

A LITURGY FOR THE
Keeping of Bees

TOGETHER: **We thank you, O God, for the blessing of bees,**
LEADER: for the wonder of their work, for the sweetness
of their offerings, and the delight of their harvest.
PEOPLE: **We thank you, O God, for the industry of the hive,**
which is like a picture of the kingdom of heaven,
always at work, in ten million places, unseen.

We thank you too for the small comedy of the creatures,
    for the humor of their constant severity,
    for the buzz and the bumbling of bees
in flight, for the sight of bees bending slender stalks
to harvest in the blooms, their feet shod in bristling boots
of gold, their backs fuzzed with bright yellow dust
that is the color of joy made visible.
So varied are your creatures, O God!
So wise your creations!

For the blessing of bees we thank you:
for their bright and varied stripes, for the wisdom
of their queen, and for the potent sting you have
granted them to guard the life of the hive against the harms
of a nature now fallen and hostile.

We thank you for imbuing them with an ingenuity
of architecture to build the perfect geometry of the comb,

    a golden cathedral that cannot be accounted an accident.

We thank you, O God,
for the miracle of bees in their labors,

    For their tireless industry—may it inspire us to serve;
    for their generosity—may we also produce enough to share.

Bless these, your creatures,
which you have given into the service of your image bearers.
May they be fruitful.

Bless these, your creatures,
May their honey be plentiful and sweet.
May they find in fields of clover and wild bloom

    a bountiful harvest of nectars,
that we might gladly share the abundance of their labors,
delighting in the sustenance and small pleasures
you have provided us through them.

Bless these bees, O God, and bless their keepers.
For all creatures are yours, bee and keeper alike.
Together may our co-labors resound to your praise and glory.

Amen.

A LITURGY FOR THE
Washing of Windows

LEADER: Ah, bright clarity of Christ,
whose light illumines our deep shadows,
whose glowing grace seeks out
    the cobwebbed corners of our souls,
whose luminous and loving presence
    fills all surrendered spaces
so that warmth and radiance abound,
PEOPLE: **meet us now in the washing of windows.**

As we labor to cleanse glass panes
of grimes smeared and blearing,
call us to consider, O Lord of light,
the same work of your Word and of your Spirit,
    ever cleansing our hearts,
    our inclinations,
    our habits,
of such stain as would block
the passage of your light through our lives.

Meet us now, O Lord, in the washing of windows.

In this small toil, call us to contemplate
    how the glass is not set in the window frame
    in order to be seen,
    but to be seen *through*.
Then show us how our lives also have been fitted
to their various frames in times and places of your choosing
    that your glory might in those places be evidenced.

Meet us now, O Lord, in the washing of windows.

Your children are the windows
through which the world sees you best.
Ever cleanse and sanctify us therefore,
not that we might be noticed for our virtues,
but that your light through us might
be ever more clearly witnessed,
your radiance and your beauty
unclouded by our sin.

Meet us now, O Lord, in the washing of windows.
Meet us and make of us more fitting casements
for the coursings of your eternal light.

Amen.

A LITURGY FOR
Home Repairs

For the blessings of this dwelling, O Lord:
    for the fast foundation,
    for the roof stretched overhead
        as a sheltering canopy,
    for the luxury and security
        of windows and doors,
    for these strong walls
        staying wind and weather,
    for comforts of floor and furniture,
        of heating and cooling, of fresh running
        water and electrical wiring,
and for all fixtures, appliances, and conveniences that make
our lives here less toilsome, we give you thanks, O Lord,
acknowledging that all provision is your provision.

This place is a gift.
The sharing of life within these walls is a gift.

And so the necessary investment of time and resource
toward the maintenance and repair of this dwelling
need not be regarded as a burden, but as a good stewardship
and a glad opportunity.

Give grace therefore that I might now
perform the task before me, not in grudging irritation,
but in gentleness and generosity of spirit, as a caretaker
of your blessings, and as an act of loving service to all family,
friends, or strangers who will shelter here or enjoy
fellowship beneath this roof.

In the midst of these labors, grant me
    practical wisdom to perceive problems,
    imagination to consider their solutions,
    and skill to remedy them.
Give me also humility and discernment, that I might know
when a task is beyond my ability, and ask for help.

Guide my hands in these endeavors, O Lord,
and yet even more, I pray that you would shape my heart
in the doing of them, that as I labor to repair this dwelling,
you would be ever at work within me, your Spirit revealing
and repairing my own places
    of brokenness, ungratefulness, shame, and pride,
and so making me an ever more fit habitation
    for the indwelling Christ,
    and a truer citizen
    of the coming kingdom.

Amen.

A LITURGY FOR
Students & Scholars

May I learn to love learning, O Lord, for the world is yours,
and all things in it speak —each in their way—of you:
> of your mind,
> your designs,
> your artistry,
> your power,
> your unfolding purpose.

All knowledge is your knowledge.
All wisdom your wisdom.

Therefore, as I apply myself to learning,
may I be mindful that all created things
are your creative expression, that all stories
are held within your greater story,
and that all disciplines of order and design
are a chasing after your thoughts—
so that greater mastery of these subjects
will yield ever greater knowledge of the
symmetry and wonder of your ways.

Along this journey, O Great Architect of Life and Beauty,
bless me with teachers who are passionate about the subjects
they teach, and with mentors who will take joy
in awakening in me a fierce love for those parts of your creation
and your story that they have already learned to love well.

As I apply myself even to those subjects
that I might at first find tedious,
reward my efforts with
    new insights,
    fresh inspiration,
    small epiphanies,
and with the firm conviction that you
are at work in my heart in all circumstances,
not only broadening my knowledge,
but also shaping my heart
by patience, endurance, and discipline
that I might mature to more fitly and humbly
serve the purposes of your great kingdom.

Give me a deepening knowledge of truth and a finer
discernment of the ideas I encounter in my studies.
Guard my mind always against error,
and guard also my heart against the temptation
to compare my own performance to the work of my peers,
and so to fall into either of the twin traps of shame or pride.

Grant instead that I might happily steward what scholarly gifts
you have apportioned me, and that I might do so as means
of preparing myself for service to you and to others,
my identity drawn from your love and forgiveness,
and not from my grades or accolades here.

Open, O Lord, as you will, the paths of my life in the days yet
to come. Use my studies to further shape my vision of what my
place and call in this world might be. Begin to show me where
my own deep gladness and the world's deep need might meet.
And in that light, let me be mindful not only of my studies, but
also mindful of the needs of my peers and even of my teachers.
Let me respond with mercy to the failings of others.

Let me be in this school, even in small ways,
a bearer of love and light and reconciliation;
which is to say, let me in humility be your child.

God grant this child discernment and wisdom.
     Guard me from error.
God grant this child knowledge and understanding.
     Lead me to truth.
God bless the labors of this new season.
     Shape me for your service.

Amen.

A LITURGY FOR
Waiters & Waitresses

Give grace this day, O Lord.
   I will probably need it.
For my work here has taught me that people can be unkind.

Some customers will receive my services gratefully,
engaging me with a cheerful friendliness
and making a point to show their thankfulness.
What a joy it is to serve them!

But others will make my day difficult,
going out of their ways to be punitive and demeaning,
meeting any kindness with rebuff, treating me like an object,
taking out on me whatever frustrations or disappointments
gnaw at their own hearts.

Give me grace to wait those tables, O God!

Let my services to all customers in this upcoming shift
be rendered as conscious acts of love to you, O Lord,
   without regard for their varied responses,
   and without expectations of their praise.

Give me your grace to lavish upon even the rude and ungrateful,
that I would learn to imitate your constant mercies
and your prodigal love relentlessly extended

 even to my own inconstant heart, O my King.

Let me serve joyfully,
knowing that every act of service offered in your name
is received by you and will have its eternal reward—

 even those acts of kindness offered

 to ungrateful customers in a restaurant.
So let me see today, O Lord, how your eternity
intersects my service here.

Now receive these, my acts of worship.

Amen.

A LITURGY FOR
First Responders

O God who shrank not from danger
but willingly entered the chaos of our world, walk
with me now as I enter the hard moments of others.

As I rush into flickering vignettes
of fear and loss,
may I carry into them your presence,
your comfort, your peace.
Do not let my adrenaline
overmaster my empathy.
May those whose lives
are overturned by emergency
find in their interactions with me
their distresses calmed, their burdens lightened.

As I assess and act, let my heart be always guided by mercy,
    my mind by right judgment,
    and my hands by your wisdom,
that by all means my presence in another person's moment
of pain or confusion might mark the beginning of your
movement to redeem the disruption of their lives.

And in those situations where my strength or skill
is not enough to aid or save, when loss or harm proves
irreparable, let me neither rage against you nor against
my own limits, O Lord, but let me instead find humility
to trust your sovereignty,
and to comfort others however I can.

I would be a bearer of your peace,
but let me also learn to rest my own heart in it,
that at the end of each shift
I might return home not shaken and distracted,
but able to be fully present for those who need me
not just in the discord of one dire moment,

    but daily through the slow and necessary lifelong work
    of deep fellowship and nurturing and love.

Amen.

A LITURGY FOR
Medical Providers

O Christ Our Healer,

There is no end to malady, sickness, injury, and disease
in this broken world, so there is no end to the line
of hurting people who daily need my tending.

Therefore give me grace, O God, that I might be generous
with my kindness, and that in this healing and care-taking
vocation my hands might become an extension of your hands,
and my service a conduit for your mercy.

For it is often not an easy place to be—
    so near to suffering, to injury, to pain,
    to emergency and fear and confusion,
    and sometimes even to dying and
    death and grief—
but I believe it is exactly the sort of place
you would be, O Lord, amongst those who hurt.
So let my practice of medicine be centered
    in an understanding of your heart.

Let me practice medicine because you are a healing God
    who feels compassion and extends mercy.
Let me practice medicine because you are near to those
    who are in need, to those who face grief and loss.
Let me practice medicine as a willing servant
    of your redemption, pushing back—
    by means of my vocation—the effects of the fall.
Let my presence in this place lend a human face
    to your compassion.

Even when my schedule is crammed with appointments,
rounds, or duties, let me never view my patients
as mere tasks on a to-do list. Give me grace instead
to be always—even in our brief encounters—attentive and
responsive to the hearts of human beings made in your image.

Let me extend kindness and mercy even to those
    who are too angry, frightened, bitter, or in pain
    to respond with anything but venom.
Let me especially love them, for they suffer—
    even more than from physical ailment—from a lack of
    understanding or experience of your overwhelming grace
    and mercy and love. Let their time with me be to them a
    taste that might awaken a hopeful hunger in their hearts.

I can do none of these things on my own.
Apart from your grace, I have no grace to give.
So give me your grace in greater measure, O Lord.

Let me find also, in the midst of such constant need,
a rhythm of service and rest that will enable my own soul
to be tended and nourished—that in the time I spend with
patients I will have a deeper repository of patience
and kindness to share with them.

Teach me how better to balance my duties
and my days, so that this work would not make me
absent from the lives of my family and friends and church.
Let me be well-woven into those communities and
relationships, enjoying ample time with them,
being available to them, and caring for their needs
even as I allow them to care for mine.

Let me never be so consumed by my vocation
that those closest to me suffer negligence.

**THE CLOSING SECTION MAY BE EXCERPTED
FOR USE AS A SHORTER LITURGY.**

I would not just be
    a doctor or
    a nurse or
    a medical provider, O God.
I would be a minister of your healing and compassion
    at work in your world.
I would be a living witness of your love expressed
    in a practical care of people.
I would be your disciple in this place, at this time,
    among these people.

So give grace, Lord Christ. Give me grace this day and all days,
that I might serve you well by loving and serving others in this
healing trade, ever laboring in view of that day when your
kingdom will be fully realized, at the great mending of the
world, at the great ending of all ills.

Let me play a small part in that great work, today.

Amen.

A LITURGY BEFORE
Taking the Stage

What have I to offer here that might sustain
the souls of others? Alone I have little more to show
beneath this scrutiny of lights than
    my own pride and insecurity,
    my craving for praise,
    and my fear of rejection.

Rather, let me offer something greater in this place, O Christ.
As I step onto this stage, meet me
    amidst the wreckage of my ego and my woundedness,
    and through me give what I alone cannot.

I offer you all that I have:
    my talents,
    my training,
    the years spent honing and crafting and creating,
    my passions,
    my personality,
    my history,
    the many sacrifices I and others
        have made in order for me to be here.
I give you even my brokenness, of which I am also a steward.

I offer now these incomplete and insufficient provisions,
remembering how you, in your days among us, twice blessed
inadequate offerings, fashioning them into miraculous feasts
that would sustain crowds in their hard journeys.

I pray that you would likewise receive and bless and multiply
my own meager gifts, Jesus, for the benefit of all who have
gathered here. Let these humble elements, in your hands,
become a true nourishment for those who hunger for you.
And for those who have not yet wakened
to their deepest hungers, let my brief service to them
be like the opening of a window through which
the breezes of a far country might blow,
stirring eternal longings to life.

Take this tiny heap of my talents and my brokenness alike,
    this jumble of what is best and worst in me,
and meld it to the greater work of your Spirit,
using each facet as you will, so that,
even as sunlight coursing through a cracked prism,
your grace might somehow be revealed upon this stage
    in whatever gloried
    and peculiar patterns
you have fashioned me to display.

Amen.

A LITURGY FOR
Fiction Writers

WRITERS: **Lord, let me love this world into being.**
LEADER: Even as you, in the infinite poetry
of your thoughts and the inexhaustible joy
of your love, spoke a universe into existence,
into life, into the complex motion of its myriad
particulars, so grant the grace that I might trace
by my thoughts and words the echoes of some
infinite pattern of your creation.

Take these my small offerings:
> my pen,
> my paper,
> my words,
> my willingness
to be still and present.

Fill my imagination.
Be to me both fire and wonder,
> inspiration and guide.

Take these my small offerings.
Take and multiply them into a story that might stir
or salve, that might shape or strengthen, that might name
hidden wounds or secret hopes, that might open hearts to your
mysteries. May your Holy Spirit meet me in the process
of creation, for even as you called into being all things
from nothing, so would I now step into the nothingness
of an empty page, trusting that your Spirit might be manifest
in this act of faith and stewardship.

Lord, let me love this world into being,
and let me love each of the characters I create,
    even those who choose to harm, who choose
    their own pride, their own strength, their
    own glory above what is right and good and
    true; let me love even those who turn from
    righteousness, who eschew grace.

May I allow them the dignity to become themselves
within the world I have created, and may I not impose my own
will upon these creations, but leave room for them to make
real choices of consequence to themselves and others.
May they have something like a breath of life in them,
and not be the shriveled fruit of my own moralizing.

Shape me by these labors.
May I return from my sojourn in this world
of the imagined, made—by the long practice of empathy—
more fit for acts of mercy and service

in this true world of your creation.

Lord, let me love the reader,
ever writing for their good,
writing words that might,

in the employ of your Spirit,
bring life and hope and conviction.

And when I have written lines that are but
my own vain ramblings, or when I am too enamored
of my own cleverness, grant me the humility and the courage
to make the hard choices, to amputate my own ego.
Reveal these deficiencies to me before I send my words
out into the world, that I might not add to the noise.

But if I do, may it please you by your grace
to turn my darkness to light so that even the fruits
of my pride and insecurity would be redeemed
for the good of your people and the furtherance
of your kingdom and the glory of your name.

Lord, let me love this world into being
because you are the author of stories

    within stories within stories and of poetry

    within all of creation

and you have made us lovers and stewards of this same gift.
We who live out our small stories within your greater story
would also tell, by your grace, such stories
as would somehow awaken hearts

    to wonder,

    to beauty,

    to truth,

    to love.

Lord, let me love this world into being.
Oh Spirit of God, be active!
Lord, let me love this world into being.
Oh Spirit of God, breathe life!
Lord, let me love this world into being.
Oh Spirit of God,

    brood over the waters

    of my finite imagination!

Call new worlds and stories into being.
Oh Spirit of God, breathe life!

A LITURGY FOR
Changing Diapers I

Heavenly Father,
in such menial moments as this—the changing of a diaper—
I would remember this truth:

    My unseen labors are not lost, for it is these
    repeated acts of small sacrifice that—
    like bright, ragged patches—
    are slowly being sewn into a quilt of
    lovingkindness that swaddles this child.

I am not just changing a diaper.
By love and service I am tending a budding heart that,
rooted early in such grace-filled devotion,
might one day be more readily-inclined to bow
to your compassionate conviction—knowing itself then
as both a receptacle and a reservoir of heavenly grace.

So this little act of diapering—
though in form sometimes felt as base drudgery—
might be better described as one of ten thousand acts
by which I am actively creating a culture
of compassionate service and selfless love to shape
the life of this family and this beloved child.

So take this unremarkable act of necessary
service, O Christ, and in your economy let it be multiplied
into that greater outworking of worship and of faith,
a true investment in the incremental
advance of your kingdom across generations.

Open my eyes that I might see this act for what it is
from the fixed vantage of eternity, O Lord—
how the changing of a diaper might sit upstream
        of the changing of a heart;
how the changing of a heart might sit upstream
        of the changing of the world.

Amen.

A LITURGY FOR
Changing Diapers II

FOR THERE ARE MANY DIAPERS THAT MUST BE CHANGED. . .

Ah Lord, what a mess we sometimes make of our lives!
What a tragic comedy is even our most sincere attempt
        to merit righteousness on our own.

We are no more able to render ourselves holy
than is this infant to keep itself unsoiled.

I am as dependent upon your grace
    and your own righteousness, O Christ,
    to justify and make me clean,
as this little one is dependent upon me to wash
    the residue of filth from its skin, wrapping it
    again in soft and freshly-laundered garments.

Let me not be frustrated
    by the constant repetition
    of this necessary act
    on behalf of a child.

Rather, let the daily doing of this
    be a reminder to me,
    of the constant cleansing and covering
    of my own sin, that I—helpless as this babe
    and more often in need—
    enjoy in the active mercies of Christ.

Amen.

A LITURGY FOR THOSE WHO WORK
In Wood & Stone & Metal & Clay

O God who in your good providence did deposit
in this world treasuries of metal and wood, stone and clay—
that we who are created in your image might
from those materials make and build and craft
objects and structures both beautiful and useful,
for the meeting of physical needs and for
the nurturing of soul and spirit—quicken now
    my hands, my ability, my knowledge,
and bless this work of creation that
by my labors I might craft a thing that sings
with the very substance of my hope.

I am here to rehearse the New Creation
in the making of this thing.

Breathe, O God, into my lifeless works
that they might somehow hold in their feeble forms
such angles and fragments and rumors
of the fire of the glory that is already made ready and waiting
to burst forth from the seams of creation's old garment—
when you but speak the word—
and all things sin-soaked and subject to futility
will be suddenly unsodden and revealed in their

truer forms in a new turning of the light,
now resurrected, now shed of
the great groan of the world, now displaying
in full measure the glory they were intended
to hold at their first crafting.

I am here to rehearse the New Creation
in the making of this thing.

Listen, all who labor—
    and my own hands and heart also—Hear!
Hear heaven's tidings now tolled as hammer
    rings, saw strums, and chisel strikes:
The hours and years you spend in this toil of mastering
your imperfect crafts—
    for joy in the nature and the working
        of these good elements;
    for joy in the beauty of the things created;
    for knowledge of God's good pleasure
    at the evidence of his image reflected in us, and of
    our images reflected in what we make; for expression
    of love in this slow and obedient fashioning
    of pleasing and durable items
        to do good service to generations;
    and for the offering of arts and
    eloquent objects which whisper to the

souls of their beholders stirrings of
eternal things that words cannot convey—

To all who traffic in the crafting of such elements,
    hear these tidings:

Those hours and labors are not lost!

What you have worked is more than it
now seems. The economy of creation is
backloaded and sits on springs. What you
have made will one day be unveiled, unleashed,
take wing, or glow with glory coursing from
that cracked chrysalis you had fashioned in
defiance of the deep shadows of this age—
and in that turning of the page we will raise
our voices in chorus and say:

    In defiance of the curse, we had been
    rehearsing all along the New Creation
    in the making of these things.

So now, Creator Spirit, unto that day,
quicken my hands; enliven my imagination.
Mediate my labor; offer inspiration.
With intention, in this shaping, may I love well

those who in the end will benefit by the thing
well-made and useful for their journey.

Accept this undertaking. May my making
now be rendered as an act of worship, O Lord,
that the care with which I craft this thing to
be both beautiful and lasting should stand in
affirmation of your covenantal acts.

And so may the thing I here create,
      even in its imperfection,
yet be an object bearing witness to the promise
that all things will be made new, a firstfruits
offering to you, from my own hand.

Amen.

A LITURGY FOR THE
Labors of Community

LEADER: Our lives are so small, O Lord,
PEOPLE: **Our vision so limited,**
Our courage so frail,
Our hours so fleeting.
Therefore give us grace and guidance for the journey ahead.

We are gathered here because we believe
that we are called together into a work
we cannot yet know the fullness of.
**Still, we trust the voice of
the One who has called us.**

And so we offer to you, O God, these things:
Our dreams, our plans, our vision.
Shape them as You will.
Our moments and our gifts.
May they be invested toward bright, eternal ends.

Richly bless the work before us, Father.
Shepherd us well lest we grow enamored
    of our own accomplishment
    or entrenched in old habit.

Instead let us listen for Your voice,
our hearts ever open to the quiet beckonings
of Your Spirit in this endeavor.
Let us in true humility and poverty of
spirit remain ever ready to move at the
impulse of your love in paths of your design.

You alone, O God,
by your gracious and life-giving Spirit
have power to knit our imperfect hearts,
        our weaknesses, our strengths,
        our stories, and our gifts, one to another.
Unite Your people and multiply
our meager offerings, O Lord,
that all might resound to Your glory.

May our acts of service and creation,
frail and wanting as they are,
be met and multiplied by the mysterious
workings of Your Spirit
who weaves all things together
toward a redemption more good and glorious
than we yet have eyes to see,
or courage to hope for.

May our love and our labors
now echo your love and
your labors, O Lord.

Let all that we do here,
    in these our brief lives,
    in this our brief moment to love,
    in this the work you have ordained
        for this community,
flower in winsome and beautiful foretaste
    of greater glories yet to come.

O Spirit of God,
    now shape our hearts.
O Spirit of God,
    now guide our hands.
O Spirit of God,
    now build Your kingdom among us.

Amen.

LITURGIES OF
Creation
& Recreation

A LITURGY FOR
Arriving at the Ocean

LEADER: We praise you, O Lord, for our limits!
PEOPLE: **Limits you have given us for
our good and for your glory.**

We praise you for this blessing—
we praise you for the boundaries of our beings!
**You have made us finite creatures
that we might be held and known.**
You have made us finite creatures that we might exult
**in the infinite wonders of your beauty,
your majesty, your love, your power.**

We have traveled this day to the bounding sea, O Lord,
to the far edge of the habitable land,
as to the utter end of our own measure
and ability and strength,
**to find here reminders of your limitless
presence extended immeasurably beyond us.**

In this place may we recall our blessed smallness.

SILENCE IS KEPT.

May we on this lovely shore lay down our pretensions of power,
shedding the burdensome dreams of our own grandeur,
and may we find instead contentment in our creatureliness.
May we grasp the grace that is here so evident.
May we know solace and calm and wonder and delight,
reveling here in a rightful place as those who
    are not, and never will be, God,
but who are yet your beloved image-bearers.

We are your creatures,
    alive because your breath has filled our lungs.
We are your people,
    restored because your salvation has found us.

May we wade here in the wild waters of your presence.
May we bask here in the golden light of your love.

In this blue space of sea and sand, of seething surf
and soothing sound, center anew our restless hearts, O Lord,
that we might embrace the wonder of the created,
that we might be contented in the finitude that
moves us to rightful awe at your awesomeness,
to rightful humility at your power,
and to a rightful delight
in your benevolent affections.

May the stresses of
    obligation,
    reputation,
    and deadline
here dissolve.
May we find rest in the renewed certainty
that we need not be
    feared
    or respected
    or popular
    or successful
    or somehow perfect,
to be loved by you.

There is no striving here at the end of our limits.
Forgive our former strivings after our own righteousness,
O Lord. In our smallness let us celebrate your greatness.

In the ocean of your presence let us taste anew
the freedom of children on holiday.
Let us ride upon these waves of endless grace,
unselfconsciously delighting in the scale of a creation,
and of a creator, and of a redemption,
so much grander than ourselves.

Amen.

A LITURGY FOR
Leaving on Holiday

LEADER: O Christ Our Sabbath,
You have fashioned us to function best
in rhyming lines of work and rest;
our relaxations and recreations
like unspoken invitations
to that still greater holiday to come—
when all burdens will at last be shed
and weariness be put to bed,
and gladsome joy stretch endlessly before us.

PEOPLE: **Bless now, O Lord,**
    this happy foretaste of that good end!

Bless our pending trip here at its first christening.
Bless the days to come:
the days of duties undone,
unbuckled, unbound.
Bless our pilgrim quest for restoration!

Prepare our hearts to revel in new exploration
    of cities not our own,
      and of landscapes less familiar.

Along our way, in such places
whose contours you deliberately created,
may we pause to savor the evidences
of your diverse imagination
expressed in glories of scenery,
and in an artistry of peoples and cultures.

Waken our vision to perceive such subtle
expressions of your nature. Rouse also our hearts
that we might be quietly shaped
by those whisperings of divine beauty.

In our days away let us play together. Let us laugh together.
Let us be moved to speak such meaningful words
as ought to be spoken among family and friends.
Let us linger long at tables and drink deeply of
one another's company, enjoying each for who they are
with the steady pressures of our ordinary days now lifted.

As you called your disciples to come away with you,
retreating from the crush of crowds, pausing in their long work,
simply to rest, to reflect, to enjoy your company, your words,
your conversation, to enjoy their fellowship with one another,
so help us also, in this time of our vacation,
to carve out spaces merely to be,
    to be with you,

to be together,
to be refreshed.
Ah, how we long for that fierce freedom for
which we were created!
Let us taste of it here in our travels!

Bless our journey and our arrival.
Bless our days spent away.
And bless also our eventual passage home, that
we might return as those who have been revived,

with hopes resurrected,
delight restored,
hearts readied again for
forward movement into life,
strength renewed to shoulder once more
the meaningful labors assigned to us
in this season.

You are our rest, Jesus.
May this vacation serve your holy purposes.
May the deep enjoyment and the grand adventure of it
stir within us eternal longings, whetting our anticipation of
that best holiday celebration that will one day
encompass all days, and all of heaven and all of earth.

Amen.

A LITURGY FOR THOSE WHO
Sleep in Tents

LEADER: How fitting, O Lord, that we who were born
into journey and exile should sometimes venture from our
homes and beds, pitching tents and making camp in wild places.

PEOPLE: **How fitting to be reminded of our state as pilgrims**
whose transient homes of brick and wood and stone,
in the light of those eternal dwellings for which we long,
are no more substantial than the wind-rippled canvas
of these tents in which we pass the night.

Restore us to our truer, wilder stories, O God.
In this wilderness, may our hearts be shed
of the insulating layers of daily routines, of
the duties and comforts that distract and lull us,
of the numbing surplus of our possessions.

Here let us feel ourselves more vulnerable and in awe,
silhouetted against the backdrop of your beauty
and holiness, small beneath towering trees and
wide skies, small but known.

Restore us to our truer, wilder stories, O God.

May we find grace in the wilderness.
May we find grace in the heart of the wood,

    in the space of the fields,
    in the rising of rocks,
    in the rushing of streams,
    in the painterly dabs of wildflowers,
    in the windswept bending of wild grasses.

Here stir our hearts
to remember that grace is ever a wild thing
that laws and progress cannot tame.
May we chase your manifold mercies over
ragged hills, pursue your song through the sparse and
layered lyric of sculpted deserts, marvel at your mystery
fixed in the wheeling designs of stars overhead.
May we hear it in the coos and calls of owls and
small creatures that fidget in the night,
trace it in the leaping dance of campfire flames,
and sense it in the sweet incense of pine and leafmeal.

Restore us to our truer, wilder stories, O God.
In this place may we breathe your quickening
breath, sleeping in tents tonight, awash in this
glorious ache, sojourners stirred afresh by
distant rumors of the return of their king.
May we wake at the soft pulse of dawn to find

in the wild and whispering winds of your Spirit,
our pilgrim hearts ringing like chimes.

Fill these wilds, O Lord,
   that in your presence,
   we might be present.

Amen.

A LITURGY FOR THE ENJOYMENT OF
Bonfires in the Night

LEADER: In the brilliant designs of all created things, O God,
in the elements and the forces and the patterns,
you have embedded the poetry of your own thoughts,
so that all things in heaven and on earth,
rightly seen, are alive and shimmering with
the veiled light of your presence and power and beauty.

PEOPLE: **Open our eyes then to holy mysteries**
fixed in spark and flame and coal and burning ember.

We praise you, O God for these sparks that fly upward,
drawing our eyes to the stars and our thoughts

to the infinite reaches of space and to the One
whose infinite Spirit set those stars in motion,
and who fills all of creation,
and who is also as a burning fire
    and a consuming flame.

We praise you, O Lord, for the leaping dance of flames,
giving warmth and comfort in the cold.
As this seasoned firewood ignites, so may our own
hearts be made suitable tinder and fanned to blaze
by the breath of your Spirit.

We praise you, O God, for light in darkness,
for bonfires and beacons,
for hope and companionship
and bright waystations on our journey.

We thank you for gatherings such as this,
amongst fellow pilgrims drawn to your light.

Burn bright your mercies, O God!
Flame high your love, O Lord!
Illumine our shadows! Warm our cold hearts!
Let us live alight with holy flame.

Amen.

A LITURGY FOR
Sunsets

AS THE SUNSET BEGINS:

LEADER: We make ourselves present to delight
in your handiwork, O Lord. We make ourselves
present to revel in this unique, one-time display
of your dynamic and infinitely-faceted glory.

PEOPLE: **We praise you, O God,
for what we are about to witness,
in patterns of cloud illumined and
crossed by a play of color and light.**

You have infused your created order with
an inexplicable beauty that is inseparable from
the expression of your nature.

Open our hearts therefore,
to the work of your beauty
cast on the canvas of sky,
to the echoes of your glory
written upon this your creation.

May this meditation upon your glories not leave us unmoved.
May we receive the expression of this beauty as we would
the lavish endearments of a love letter.

Tender our hearts to receive it.

SILENCE IS KEPT FOR THE DURATION OF THE CELESTIAL DISPLAY.
AS THE LAST COLORS OF SUNSET FADE TO WESTERN DARKNESS,
AN APPROPRIATE PSALM, HYMN, OR SONG OF PRAISE MAY BE SUNG
OR RECITED.

May the patterns of your eternal beauties
be fixed in our souls, O Lord.
That the lives we lead and the words we speak
might hereafter be infused with a grace
that would show forth your beauty.

May your people be as winsome as the sunset,
O God, and give as little cause for offense,
as they carry your name, your truth,
and your love into this world.

**Our hearts and our lives
are your canvas, O Spirit of God.
We yield them to you.**

Go forth, you image bearers of God.
Go forth bearing his image
    and sharing his beauty.

Amen.

A LITURGY FOR
Stargazing

LEADER: O Great Architect of These Intricate Heavens,

We have assembled under open skies this night
to ponder your handiwork, to be moved to
wonder at the poetry of your thoughts revealed
    in endless patterns of light.

How limitless the creative power of the One
    who first scattered these starfields
    as a sower flinging bright seeds.

PEOPLE: **How fathomless the thoughts of the One**
    who named and remembers each burning star,
    and who also names and remembers each of us.

Now you, his people, lift your eyes to the
    heavens, and consider his handiworks.

SILENCE IS KEPT, AS NIGHT SKIES ARE PONDERED.

Constellations rise and descend the staircase
of the night at your command, O Lord.
Galaxies spin like dancers. Space and time
bend and bow to the gravity of your great will.

In such holy wonders,
baptize our imaginations,
that we might ever be a people shaped
by awe at your eternal power,
and a people moved to worship
by revelations of your divine nature.

Awaken our hearts now to beat
in rhythm to the dance of your creation.
Tune our ears to hear the songs
of stars in their trillion-fold choruses,
bearing witness to your glory, your power.

**Use these bright expressions of your extravagant
beauty to stoke our holy longings, whetting our
appetites afresh for all that is eternal and good.**

You made this vastness, and by
your love you placed us in it,
fixed amongst the wonders.
**So let us be stirred, O Lord, by night skies such as these,
lifting our thoughts to you, our Maker, and to the vast
and beautiful infinitude of your designs.**

O Spirit of God, draw praise from us,
    here in this cathedral of creation,
    beneath this starry dome.
**Awaken our adoration in this place
where we are so very small—**
    and yet so greatly loved.

Amen.

A LITURGY FOR THE
Watching of Storms

LEADER: In every storm there is a sermon
playing out in parable across the canvas of sky,
telling of the awesome power of one whose judgments are just,
but whose mercies are thereby all the more
    scandalous and unexpected,
and whose tender love for us
    is beyond comprehension.

PEOPLE: **Praise be to God, for his infinite mercies.**

Indeed we praise you, O Lord, that having both
might and right to crush whatever within us would
assert itself against you, you instead crushed yourself, and
by that act offered us life, taking the brunt of such
furious judgment into your own form, and shielding us
forever from what our treason so rightly deserved.

Thanks be to God, for his unmerited grace.

Now may these mighty winds, these lightning strikes,
these crashing calls of thunder, these hard rains,
    by their fierce beauty set us in awe—

their witness rightly reminding us
of that just verdict
we will never have to face,
the ferocity of these elements
an inverse testament
to the affections of the one whose
strong love has now become
     our shield against the coming storm.

✝Glory to God, for his sheltering love, extended even to us.

O Christ Who is Our Peace, cradle us now,
even as you will cradle us at that final reckoning,
calming every fear by your nearness,
as we watch with wondering eyes,
this storm-told story
     of a great judgment
     and an even greater mercy.

Amen.

A LITURGY FOR THE
First Snow

THE SNOWFALL IS OBSERVED IN REFLECTIVE SILENCE
BEFORE ALL JOIN THE LEADER IN THIS PRAYER:

PEOPLE: **O Christ, King of Snow,**
we bless you for bidding this blanket
of white to cover us in holy hush,
that our hearts might be quieted at the sight,
that we might sense
> **the emptiness of canvas**
over which your Spirit broods,
and upon which you would
> **create**
> **and recreate**
our hearts in the image of the one
> **whose word first spoke snow into existence.**

Amen.

A LITURGY BEFORE
Consuming Media

O Discerning Spirit, who alone judges all things rightly,
now be present in my mind and active in my imagination
as I prepare to engage with the claims and questions of
diverse cultures incarnated in the stories that people tell.

Let me experience mediums of art and expression,
neither as a passive consumer nor as an entertainment
glutton, but rather as one who through such works
would more fully and compassionately enter this ongoing,
human conversation of mystery and meaning,
    wonder and beauty, good and evil, sorrow
    and joy, fear and love.

All truth is your truth, O Lord, and all beauty is your beauty.
Therefore use human expressions of celebration and longing
as catalysts to draw my mind toward ever deeper insight,
my imagination into new and wondering awe,
and my heartbeat into closer rhythm with your own.

Shape my vision by your fixed precepts, and tutor me,
Holy Spirit, that I might learn to discern the difference
between those stories that are whole,

echoing the greater narrative of your redemption,
     and those that are bent or broken,
failing to trace accurately the patterns of your
eternal thoughts and so failing to name rightly the true
condition of humanity and of all creation.

Grant me wisdom to divide rightly, to separate
     form from content,
     craft from narrative,
     and meaning from emotion.
Bless me with the great discernment to be able
to celebrate the stamp of your divine image revealed
in an excellence of craft and artistry even while grieving
a paucity of meaning or hope in the same work.

Guard my mind against the old enticement
     to believe a lie simply because it is beautifully told.
Let me not be careless. Give me right conviction
to judge my own motives in that which I
approve, teaching me to be always mindful of that which I
consume, and thoughtful of the ways in which I
consume it. Impart to me keener knowledge of the
limits of my own heart in light of my own particular
brokenness, that I might choose what would
be for my flourishing and not for my harm.

And give me the grace to understand that
what causes me to stumble might bear no ill
consequence for another of your children,
so that while I am to care for my brothers
and sisters, I must also allow them,
in matters of conscience, the freedom
to sometimes choose a thing your Spirit
convicts me to refrain from.

    Even so, let my own
    freedoms in Christ never be flaunted or
    exercised in such a way as to give cause for
    confusion, temptation, or stumbling in others.

May the stories I partake of, and the ways in
which I engage with them, make me in the end
a more empathetic Christ-bearer, more
compassionate, more aware of my own
brokenness and need for grace,
better able to understand the hopes and fears
and failings of my fellow humans,
so that I might more authentically live and learn
and love among them unto the end that all of
our many stories might be more beautifully
woven into your own greater story.

Amen.

A LITURGY FOR THE
Planting of Flowers

PREPARE THE BED FOR PLANTING.ONCE THE SOIL IS PREPARED,
EACH PARTICIPANT CRADLES IN THEIR PALM ONE OF THE
UNPLANTED FLOWERS, BULBS, OR FLOWER SEEDS.

LEADER: In a world shadowed by cruelty, violence and loss,
is there good reason for the planting of flowers?

PEOPLE: **Ah, yes!**
For these bursts of color and beautiful blooms
are bright dabs of grace,
witnesses to a promise,
reminders of a spreading beauty
more eternal, and therefore stronger,
than any evil, than any grief,
than any injustice or violence.

What is the source of their beauty? From whence does it spring?

The forms of these flowers are the intentional
designs of a Creator who has not abandoned his
broken and rebellious creation, but has instead
wholly given himself to the work of redeeming it.

He has scattered the evidences
of creation's former glories across
the entire scape of heaven and earth,
and these evidences are also foretastes of the
coming redemption of all things, that those
who live in this hard time between glories
    might see and remember,
    might see and take heart,
    might see and take delight
in the extravagant beauty of bud and bloom,
knowing that these living witnesses are rumors and
reminders of a joy that will soon swallow all sorrow.

In the planting of these flowers, do we join the Creator
in his work of heralding this impending joy?

Yes. In this and in all labors of beauty and harmony,
praise and conciliation, we become God's co-workers
and faithful citizens of his kingdom,
by acts both small and great, bearing witness
to the perfect beauty that was,
to the ragged splendor that yet is,
and to the hope of the greater glory that is to come,
which is the immeasurable glory
of God revealed to us,
in the redeemed natures of all things.

PARTICPANTS HERE KNEEL AND PLANT THE SEED, BULB,
OR FLOWER THEY HAVE BEEN HOLDING.

What then is the eternal weight of these flowers?

Though our eyes yet strain to see it so, these tiny
seeds, bulbs, or velvet buds we have planted are more
substantial than all the collected evils of this groaning
world. Their color and beauty speak a truer word
than all greed and cruelty and suffering and harm.

What is the truer word spoken by these flowers?

They are like a banner planted on a hilltop,
proclaiming God's right ownership of these
lands long unjustly claimed by tyrants and
usurpers. They are a warrant and a witness,
each blossom shouting from the earth
    that death is a lie,
    that beauty and immortality
       are what we were made for.
They are heralds of a restoration that will
forever mend all sorrow and comfort all grief.
They declare a kingdom of peace,
of righteousness, of joy, of love, and of the
great joining of justice and mercy into a

splendored perfection in the person of
a king whose amaranthine wonders eternally
upwell, beautiful beyond the grasp
of human imagination.

How will these brief blooms accomplish such
mighty labors? What grace will sustain them?

Because their work is so great, we pray,
O Father, your blessing on these small
flowers. May their roots work deep,
finding rich soil. May their leaves and buds
be wakened by gentle sun and watered by
ample rain. May the strength of their fragile
beauty in bloom give pause to passers-by,
who will meet in their sweet scent and radiant
forms whisperings of grace, stirrings of the
spirit, and the awakenings of eternal hungers,
that can be met and satisfied only in you.

Let these flowers, O Lord, bear witness in their
deepest natures to eternal things.
Let our lives also, O Lord, do the same.

Amen.

A LITURGY FOR
Gardening

LEADER: O Creator who calls forth life,
May this ground, and our labors
here invested, yield good provision for
the nourishing of both body and soul.

PEOPLE: **Lord, let our labors in this garden be fruitful.
Lord, let our labors in this garden be blessed.**

As we work the soil of this garden plot—furrowing, planting,
watering, and harvesting—may such acts become to us
a living parable, a prayer acted out rather than spoken.

**Lord, let our labors in this garden be fruitful.
Lord, let our labors in this garden be blessed.**

As we co-labor with you and with your creation
to produce a beneficial harvest, may we
find in such toil a kind of rest. May this plot
of ground become a hallowed space and
these hours a sacred time for reflection, for
conversation with friends and family, and for
fellowship with you, our Creator.

Lord, let our labors in this garden be fruitful.
Lord, let our labors in this garden be blessed.

Through our tending of these your delightful creations—
vegetables and fruits, beans and berries, vines and stalks and
roots and flowers—renew our own tired hopes,
redeem our own wearied imaginations.

As we cultivate gentle order,
    training,
    pruning,
    weeding,
    and protecting,
so cultivate and train our wayward hearts,
O Lord, that rooted in you the forms of
our lives might spread in winsome witness,
maturing to bear the good fruit of grace, expressed
in acts of compassionate love.

Lord, let our labors in this garden be fruitful.
Lord, let our labors in this garden be blessed.

Walk with us now, O Lord,
in the stillness of this tilled and quiet space,
that when we venture again into the still
greater garden of your world, we might be

prepared by the long practice of your presence,
to offer our lives as a true and nourishing
provision to all who hunger for
>   mercy
>   and hope
>   and meaning,
a true and nourishing provision
to all who hunger for you.

Lord, let our labors in this garden be fruitful.
Lord, let our labors in this garden be blessed.

Amen.

A LITURGY BEFORE
Beginning a Book

Author of Life and Author of My Life,

As I begin the reading of this book,
give me a sensitivity to listen,
>   not just to the story told,
but to the responses of my own heart
to what I encounter in these pages.

What does it draw out of me?
What joy?
What longing?
What fears?
What temptation?
What hope?
What mirth?
What love of beauty?
What awe?
What wonder?
What doubt?
What faith?
What resolve?
What unfinished grief?
What untended wound?

Give me ears to hear, O Spirit of God,
what notes the reading of this story would strike
and what melody it would draw forth
from the tuned strings of my own soul.

Waste no moment in my brief years, O Lord.
Let all things, and this book as well,
    be as tools in your hands,
to shape me and make me more truly your own,
more fitly a child of the hope

of the restoration of all things in Christ
whose fullness dwells within them.

So let the honest responses
of my heart to this reading
grant new insight into the story
your grace is already telling in my own life
that I might be a more willing co-laborer
in that process.

Amen.

LAMENT UPON THE FINISHING OF A
Beloved Book

I am stirred and saddened, O Lord,
    in coming to this tale's end,
to bid farewell and return now
from my sojourn in that storied place
where longings for something more
than the life I lead were wakened.

It is in the receding glow of that small,
bright sorrow that I now linger.

Let it do its work in me,
  inviting me to dig beneath these
  fresh-stirred longings, to see
  that their roots are not at last a longing
  for the places depicted in these pages,
  but are, in truth,
  profound and holy wounds,
  yearnings for a lost garden and a more
  perfect city, where justice and righteousness
  are restored, and harms are healed, and losses
  redeemed, and love proved true,
  and earth and heaven reconciled.

What I feel is, at its heart, a homesick hope
for a place of unbroken communion
with my Creator, and with his people,
and with all of his creation.
What I most desire
is to open my eyes and find that,
for the first time in my life,
I am home and breathing
the wild winds of my native land.

So of course my heart aches
each time I receive these beautiful, distant
rumors of that far country!

Of course I do not want such a story to end,
for it has wedged open for me a way like a window,
through which I have glimpsed a vision of things
more as they will one day be than as they now are
in these hard and sorrowing lands of our exile.

Thank you, O my God,
for loving me enough
that you would rouse
my deepest desires again through story,
appointing these longings as true signposts
planted in a war-torn and cratered landscape,
reminding me that all of history is leading at last
     to a king and a kingdom,
and pointing me ever onward toward
his righteous and eternal city.

May I return now
from the world of this book
to the daily details of my own life
with truer vision and fiercer hope,
trailing with me remnants of that coming glory
I have glimpsed again
in story.

Amen.

A LITURGY FOR
Those Who Compete

There are, O Lord, eternal patterns—
fragments of the story of redemption—
etched into our competitions.

So let me be shaped by my participation
in them—in this active parable of struggle,
in this drama of things to be risked and lost
or gained, of heroics, of hope defeated, and
hope resurgent, of wars waged against
doubt and the voices in my own head, of
struggle against the elements, struggle
against the limits of my own strength and
endurance and ability, and of struggle against
a real opponent who seeks my defeat.

For these are each small echoes
of the fights that a life of long obedience
to Christ might entail.

So let the many struggles in this
competitive arena serve to form in me
a resolve that will spill

from the boundaries marked out
for this contest,
and into the ways I live out this life of
discipleship—with intentionality, and focus,
ever mindful of the clock,
and with eyes fixed on the prize,
knowing my time here will be brief and,
therefore, my choices will matter.

Though my training for this event is physical
and mental, may it also serve to shape christlike
qualities in my spirit—yielding a greater
    fortitude,
    endurance,
    faith,
    focus,
    discipline,
    and intentionality
in the ways that I live my life in your
service and for your glory, O God.

Unto that end let me strive for
excellence in form and execution,
training hard, enjoying the abilities
of the mind and body you have given me,
knowing that even in the strength

and grace and beauty and creativity of your
creatures at play, you take great pleasure.

Teach me to be
      gracious in victory,
      and gracious in defeat,
remembering that in this competitive context
I am first your emissary,
a representative of your
emerging redemption extended
even onto the fields
of competition.

Let me never love winning more
than I love those against whom I compete.
Let me care for coaches, teammates,
opponents and spectators,
remembering that, while
the stakes of this game are only temporary,
the people around me are eternal.

Give me a graciousness
to appreciate and to praise
the performances of others,
even of my opponents.

Give me grace to instantly forgive slights,
and to quickly take responsibility when my own
actions or emotions impact others. When I am
involved in the escalation of conflict, let me be
the first to ask forgiveness.

Let me model what it is to be
one fiercely focused on, and invested in,
the drama at hand,
pushing myself always toward the goal,
and yet ever extending
a humility and graciousness
in keeping with my status
as your servant, O Christ.

May your Spirit be always active in and through me,
shaping and sanctifying my heart
    even here
    in the midst of my competitions.

Amen.

LITURGIES OF

Blessing
& Celebration

A LITURGY FOR THOSE GATHERED
On the Eve of a Wedding

NOTIFY ATTENDEES IN ADVANCE THAT THIS LITURGY INCLUDES A
TIME TO SPEAK SHORT BLESSINGS FOR THE BRIDE AND GROOM,
SO THAT ANY WHO DESIRE TO DO SO MIGHT PREPARE THEIR
THOUGHTS AND WORDS BEFOREHAND.

BEST MAN: Welcome all, to this glad hour
and to this festive table!
MAID OF HONOR: Let each find their place
in this good company!

GUESTS FIND THEIR PLACES AND REMAIN STANDING
BEHIND THEIR CHAIRS.

OFFICIANT (typically a Minister or Priest):
For what reason are we gathered in this place?
ALL PRESENT: **We are gathered for a celebration!**
OFFICIANT: Why are we called to this table?
ALL PRESENT: **We are called to a feast!**
OFFICIANT: And what do we feast here?
What do we celebrate?

ALL PRESENT: **We celebrate our joy tonight,
on the eve of the wedding of** *(Bride)* **and** *(Groom)*,
and we feast our blessing of the same!

MAID OF HONOR: Now set sorrows aside,
friends, or hold them loosely for these hours.
Accept this invitation to feasting and gladness,
for it is a foretaste of that marriage sacrament
still to come.

BEST MAN: Laugh and be glad, friends,
but even in joy do not hide the welling of your
meaningful tears if they be born of love for this
bride and for this groom.

ALL PRESENT: **Amen.**

OFFICIANT: Now may our sovereign
Lord, who has purposefully twined
all of our many stories together
in the love of *(Bride)* and *(Groom)*,
be present in this hour and at this table,
that our feasting and our fellowship,
indeed that our very gladness, might resound
as a praise of his enduring goodness!

ALL PRESENT: **Amen!**

OFFICIANT: Be seated for this happy feast.

ALL TAKE THEIR SEATS, FILLING THEIR GLASSES WITH WHATEVER
BEVERAGE THEY CHOOSE AS THE GROOM AND BRIDE CONTINUE.

GROOM: You are invited here as those who have
long loved us, guiding, nurturing, and shaping *(Bride)*
and me, proving yourselves faithful in a thousand ways.
BRIDE: You are here as the generations who have cared for
and carried us from the times of our births until now.
And you are here as the brothers and sisters and friends who
have walked beside us, the ones who have laughed
and wept with us, the ones who knew us best.
GROOM: Until we found each other.

HERE THE GROOM MAY KISS HIS BRIDE-TO-BE
ON THE HAND OR FOREHEAD.

GROOM: You have, all of you, each in your ways,
been vital to our stories as they have unfolded,
as they have brought my bride and me, by God's providence,
to this very night, gathered in love here in this holy moment—
BRIDE: a moment carved out to savor your company,
marking together this last of our shared hours
in this chapter of our lives, before my groom and I
are vowed to one another, from tomorrow till life's end.

ALL PRESENT: **May the days of your lives together
be many and blessed! May the sharing of your lives
together be sweet! May you be to each other true lovers,
faithful friends, and best companions!**

OFFICIANT: May your love for one another,
(Bride) and *(Groom)*, flow always from the
inexhaustible fountainhead of the greater love
of God. And may you grow together in the
compassion of Christ, each now as the primary
human advocate of his mercies for the other;
each now as the most constant conduit of his
grace and love extended to the other.
ALL PRESENT: **Amen.**

OFFICIANT: Now we direct our hearts to God,
petitioning his blessings on your behalf:
FATHER OF THE GROOM: In an age hostile to the keeping
of promises, may you stand side-by-side, defending always
and with great passion your holy pledge to one another;
and may your souls be shaped, through joy and sorrow alike,
by long obedience to those good promises.
MOTHER OF THE GROOM: May your love for one another
overflow in blessing to all who have the joy of knowing you.
May the world be better loved because of your passion
for each other. May the flame of your love never wane,

but burn ever fiercer across the years, that even in old age
you would remain wellsprings of one another's delight.
MOTHER OF THE BRIDE: May your home be ever a haven
of tenderness. May you never retreat from one another
in your woundedness. Rather, when you feel most vulnerable,
when you feel most hurt, may you learn in those moments
most of all, to lean in to your love, holding it all the more
precious for the sacrifices it requires.
FATHER OF THE BRIDE: May your shared story be one of
courage and creativity, of conviction and compassion
as you co-labor in the light of that better kingdom
of which you are true citizens. Along your path through
this life, may you build together bright beacons,
that those generations still to follow might one day
walk in your illuminated footprints toward that eternal city.

ANY PRESENT WHO SO DESIRE MAY NOW SPEAK ALOUD OTHER
SHORT BLESSINGS FOR THE BRIDE AND GROOM.

THE OFFICIANT NOW MAKES THE FOLLOWING SHORT ADDRESS:

OFFICIANT: In the span of the history of this world, your
marriage will last only for a short season, and yet, how fraught
with meaning it might be! For this is the holy time apportioned
for you to prove the faithfulness of God, and to display his
glories in the unique invention of your marriage.

So spend this short season well. Spend each of your
shared moments and hours. Spend them in wondering delight
at the blessings of God. Spend them in passioned pursuit of
Christ, in fellowship with his people, in constant love and
service to one another and to your family, your neighbors,
your community.

Let your lives together be woven as a parable of hope
in a world desperate for visible evidences that the eternal
longing for redemption and reconciliation is real,
that the deep ache for beauty might yet lead to something
lasting, and that the glorious rumors of divine love
and mercy are true.

ALL PRESENT: **May your marriage flourish
into a living witness of these things.
Amen.**

THE BRIDE AND GROOM RAISE THEIR GLASSES

GROOM: Here we drink to the love of our families,
and to the faithfulness of our friends.
BRIDE: May our Heavenly Father richly bless each of you,
for our debts to you are greater than we can repay.

BRIDE AND GROOM HEARTILY DRINK.

ALL OTHERS PRESENT THEN RAISE THEIR GLASSES.

ALL PRESENT: **Here we drink to our deep love
of both of you, and for the joy we share this hour
at the joining of your hearts! May the Spirit of God
dwell richly within you and rest upon you
all the days of your lives.**

**May the comforting presence of Christ and the
many blessings of the Father always be yours!**

ALL PRESENT DRINK IN GLAD TOAST TO THE BRIDE AND GROOM.

OFFICIANT: Now friends—and with and in the blessing
of God—let us feast and celebrate together.
ALL PRESENT: **Amen! Let us feast and be glad!**

A LITURGY TO
Begin a Purposeful Gathering

LEADER: And so are we gathered here,
uniquely in all of history, we particular
people in this singular time and place.
PEOPLE: **Accomplish your purposes
among us, O God.**
Tune our hearts to the voice of your Spirit.

**Wake us to be present to you and to one
another in these shared hours we are given.**
For it is you, O Lord, who have
so gathered us from our various places,
**and you alone who know our hearts
and our needs.**

Among us are some who arrive anxious, some
who are lonely, some who suffer pain or sorrow.
**May we in our joys find grace to enter the
sorrows of others.**

Among us are some who arrive rejoicing,
hearts made light by good news, good health,
glad anticipation.
**May we in our sorrows find grace to embrace
the joys of others.**

Let us prize these moments
and care for one another deeply
—for each of us,
    and our relationships to one another, are
    precious and fleeting.
Amen.

Let us prize these moments
and care for one another deeply
—for each of us,
>   and our relationships to one another, are
>   precious and eternal.

Amen.

TOGETHER: **Breathe upon our gathering,
O Spirit of God.**
Grant each of us a place to humbly receive and
to faithfully serve, that we might know in this
brief gathering a foretaste of that greater
communion yet to come.

O Father, enlarge our hearts.
O Spirit, expand our vision.
O Christ, establish your kingdom among us.
Be at work even now, O Lord.
May your will, in us, in these hours,
be accomplished.

Amen.

A LITURGY FOR
Feasting with Friends

CELEBRANT: To gather joyfully is indeed a serious affair,
   for feasting and all enjoyments gratefully taken are,
   at their heart, acts of war.
PEOPLE: **In celebrating this feast**
we declare that
   evil and death,
   suffering and loss,
   sorrow and tears,
will not have the final word.

But the joy of fellowship, and the welcome and comfort
of friends new and old, and the celebration of these blessings
of food and drink and conversation and laughter are the true
evidences of things eternal, and are the first fruits of that
great glad joy that is to come and that will be unending.

So let our feast this day be joined
to those sure victories secured by Christ,
Let it be to us now a delight, and a glad
foretaste of his eternal kingdom.
Bless us, O Lord, in this feast.

Bless us, O Lord, as we linger over our cups, and over this table
laden with good things, as we relish the delights of varied
texture and flavor, of aromas and savory spices, of dishes
prepared as acts of love and blessing, of sweet delights
made sweeter by the communion of saints.

May this shared meal, and our pleasure in it,
bear witness against the artifice and deceptions
of the prince of the darkness that would blind
this world to hope.
**May it strike at the root of the lie that would drain life of
meaning, and the world of joy, and suffering of redemption.**

May this our feast fall like a great hammer blow
against that brittle night,
shattering the gloom, reawakening our hearts,
stirring our imaginations, focusing our vision
on the kingdom of heaven that is to come,
on the kingdom that is promised,
on the kingdom that is already, indeed, among us,
For the resurrection of all good things
     has already joyfully begun.

ALL PARTICIPANTS NOW LIFT THEIR GLASSES OR CUPS.

May this feast be an echo of that great Supper of the Lamb,
a foreshadowing of the great celebration
**   that awaits the children of God.**

Where two or more of us are gathered, O Lord,
there you have promised to be.
And here we are.
And so, here are you. Take joy, O King, in this our feast.
Take joy, O King!

GLASSES ARE CLINKED WITH CELEBRATORY CHIME,
AND PARTICIPANTS IN THE FEAST SAVOR A DRINK,
ADMONISHING ONE ANOTHER HEARTILY
WITH THESE SINCERE WORDS:

Take joy!
CELEBRANT: All will be well!

PARTICIPANTS TAKE UP THE CRY:

All will be well!
Nothing good and right and true will be lost
forever. All good things will be restored.
Feast and be reminded! Take joy, little flock.
Take joy! Let battle be joined!
Let battle be joined!

Now you who are loved by the Father, prepare your hearts
and give yourselves wholly to this celebration of joy,
to the glad company of saints, to the comforting fellowship
of the Spirit, and to the abiding presence of Christ
who is seated among us both as our host and as our
honored guest, and still yet as our conquering king.
Amen.

In the name of the Father, the Son, and the Holy Spirit,
take seat, take feast, take delight!

A LITURGY FOR
Moving Into a New Home

LEADER: We thank you for this new home, O Lord, for the shelter
it will provide, for the moments of life that will be shared within it.
PEOPLE: **We thank you for this our new home
and we welcome you here.**

Dwell with us in this place, O Lord.
Dwell among us in these spaces, in these rooms.
Be present at this table as we eat together.
Be present as we rise in the morning and lie down at night.
Be present in our work here. Be present in our play.

**May your Spirit inhabit this home, making of it a
sanctuary where hearts and lives are knit together,**
where bonds of love are strengthened,
where mercy is learned and practiced.

May this our home be a harbor of anchorage and refuge,
**and a haven from which we journey forth
to do your work in your world.**
May it be a garden of nourishment in which our roots go deep
that we might bear fruit for the nourishing of others.

May this our new home be a place of knowing
and of being known,
a place of shared tears and laughter;
a place where forgiveness is easily asked and granted,
and wounds are quickly healed;
a place of meaningful conversation, of words not left unsaid;
a place of joining, of becoming, of creating, and reflecting;
a place where our diverse gifts are named and appreciated;
where we learn to serve one another
and to serve our neighbors as well;
**a place where our stories are forever twined
by true affections.**

Grant also, O Lord, that our days lived gratefully within
these temporary walls, enjoying these momentary fellowships,

would serve to awaken within us a restless longing for our
truer home. Incline our hearts ever toward the glories
of that better city, built by you, O God—
a city whose blessings are neverending,
and whose fellowships are eternally unbroken.

Amen.

A LITURGY TO MARK THE FIRST
Hearthfire of the Season

PARTICIPANTS SHOULD PREPARE THE FIRE FOR LIGHTING
BEFORE BEGINNING. IF IT IS A WOOD-BURNING FIREPLACE,
EACH MAY KEEP ONE SMALL TWIG OR STICK IN HAND.

LEADER: You have appointed us to
diverse fields, O Lord, calling us to venture
forth and labor in them unto your glory.
But you have also given us warm spaces of
providence and sustenance to return to, wherein
our hearts might rest and flourish.
PEOPLE: **Bless then this hearth, O Lord,**
and bless the gatherings that will happen
around it in the coming season.

THE FIRE IS KINDLED AND OBSERVED FOR A TIME
IN THOUGHTFUL SILENCE.

May this hearth be to us a port in the storm,
a cheering beacon, and a place of fellowship
marked by the consolation of your Spirit.

THE FOLLOWING MAY BE READ BY VARIOUS PARTICIPANTS IN TURN,
ONE LINE EACH AFTERWARDS LAYING THEIR TWIGS UPON THE FIRE.

May it be a place of celebration,
Of conversation, and of caring,
Of the sharing and bearing of burdens,
Of the multiplication of joys,
Of light in the darkness and warmth in the cold.
May it be a place of prayers and hopes,
Of plans and quiet considerations.
A place of shared stories and of good dreams.

O God of counsel and comfort, may this hearth be a holy place
where our souls are deepened by fellowship and reflection,
even as harbors are dredged to create deeper, fairer havens.

Grant us grace to savor this season as we live it together,
that in later days the memory of this place and these times
will linger sweetly, shaping our lives, our words, our deeds.

May the comfort and fellowship of this hearth be so kindled in our own hearts, O Lord, that as we journey outward from this place, even in seasons of cold and darkness, we will do so always carrying the warmth of your love, and the light of your mercies.

Amen.

A LITURGY TO MARK THE START OF THE
Christmas Season

LEADER: As we prepare our house for the coming Christmas season, we would also prepare our hearts for the returning Christ.
PEOPLE: **You came once for your people, O Lord, and you will come for us again.**

Though there was no room at the inn
to receive you upon your first arrival,
**We would prepare you room
here in our hearts
and here in our home, Lord Christ.**

As we decorate and celebrate, we do so to mark the memory of your redemptive movement into our broken world, O God.

Our glittering ornaments and Christmas trees,
Our festive carols, our sumptuous feasts—
By these small tokens we affirm that something amazing
has happened in time and space—
that God, on a particular night, in a particular place, so many
years ago, was born to us, an infant King, our Prince of Peace.

Our wreaths and ribbons and colored lights, our giving of gifts, our
parties with friends—these have never been ends in themselves.
They are but small ways in which we repeat that sounding
joy first proclaimed by angels in the skies near Bethlehem.

In view of such great tidings of love announced
to us, and to all people, how can we not be moved
to praise and celebration in this Christmas season?
As we decorate our tree, and as we feast and laugh
and sing together, we are rehearsing our coming joy!
We are making ready to receive the one
who has already, with open arms, received us!
We would prepare you room here in our hearts
and here in our home, Lord Christ.
Now we celebrate your first coming, Immanuel,
even as we long for your return.
O Prince of Peace, our elder brother, return soon.
We miss you so!

Amen.

A LITURGY FOR SETTING UP A
Christmas Tree

LEADER: O Immanuel, we would find in our traditions
these reminders of the wonders of your love:

> First, let this fragrant tree, cut down
> and then raised beneath our roof,
> remind us how once upon a time,
> the High King of Heaven consented to
> be cut off from the glories that were his birthright,
> and descended instead to dwell with us
> in a broken world, beset by harm and evil.

PEOPLE: **Praise to you, Immanuel!**

> Next, let the hard wood of the trunk
> and the outstretched branches remind
> us how that same Heavenly King who
> had entered our world on that distant
> night, would soon act to redeem his
> creation and his people in it, though it
> would require the stretching out of his
> arms upon a cross of wood—his death
> for our life.

Praise to you, Immanuel!

> Then, let these evergreen boughs
> be a reminder of his mighty triumph
> over death and hell, of his resurrection
> unto a life eternal which will never fade—
> an eternal life which he has also secured
> for us. There is no greater gift!

Praise to you, Immanuel!

> Finally, as we drape the branches of this Christmas tree
> in glittering finery and sparkling lights, let us
> imagine Christ our King, seated
> upon his heavenly throne, arrayed
> in the royal raiments of his glory. And when
> at last we set the star atop the tree, let us imagine
> Christ crowned in his splendor, and all creatures
> in heaven and on earth bowing before
> him, crying "Holy! Holy! Holy!"

Glory to you, Immanuel!
> **Worthy are you, O Lamb of God,**
> **to receive all glory, honor, and praise!**

Glory to you, Lord Christ!

A LITURGY FOR
Welcoming a New Pet

LEADER: Lord and Giver of All Good Things,
PEOPLE: **You created the world and all
creatures, each wonderfully unique**
and endowed with attributes that illuminate
the poetries of your mind, your power,
your beauty, your loyalty, your sense of humor,
your playfulness, your delight.

You also created people, fashioning us in your own image,
and calling us to live ever after in right
relationship to the rest of your creation,
serving as benevolent regents
of your redemptive purposes.

With that honor you have offered us
the pleasant responsibility
of living as companions and caretakers
of our fellow creatures.

**And so it is with glad hearts that we welcome into our
home and lives this animal which you have created.**
We now bestow upon this pet the name of _____.

**Bless, O Lord, the time we are given
to share with this your unique creation.**
May we find joy in these days of
companionship with a fellow creature.

Bless this your creature, O Lord, as it enters our home.
Among us may it find nurturing care and
a sense of security that its needs will be met,
and that it will be well-treated
and never cruelly harmed.
May it never be ill-used or neglected or
have need to be anxious or in fear.

**May our love for this your creature
tender our own hearts for your purposes.**
May our attachment to this animal never be a thing
turned inward, diminishing our love for and interaction
with people in our lives, but may it work upon us
to further open our hearts to love all of your creation
more deeply and to embody that love more diligently
in our words and actions towards others.

**Shape our lives, O Lord, through our
sheltering of this new pet.**

Through our caretaking, cultivate in each of us
a heart more like that of a good shepherd,
who would always meet the needs of his or her creatures,
and in so doing, grant us fresh insight into the nature
of your own shepherd's heart towards us,
your own great delight in our companionship,
your own lavish affection for all you have made.

Amen.

A LITURGY FOR A
Yard Sale

LEADER: How easy it is, O Lord, for our lives
to become cluttered, for the spaces we inhabit
to be filled with such an overwhelming abundance of
things that we cease even to regard them.
PEOPLE: **Center our hearts again in you,
O Lord. Let us be satisfied in your love.**

How easy for us to find ourselves harried by the organizing
and tending and maintenance of things that are no longer
novel, or useful, or desired. How easy for our shelves
and drawers and closets to be filled with an accumulation of
past fashions, outmoded media, dated decor, toys and trinkets

and souvenirs, games and puzzles with missing pieces,
forgotten appliances piled in cabinets, books we'll never read
again, once-costly technologies now hopelessly obsolete.

Center our hearts again in you, O Lord.
Let us be satisfied in your love.

As we now sift such goods, weighing worth and making ready
for selling, may this culling become more than a physical act
of decluttering. May it also be for us a season of glad
examination of our own hearts and habits, of the ways in which
we have stewarded all that you have entrusted to us.

May we engage in such introspection—not so that we would be
burdened with a greater guilt at our failings—but rather so
that we would be better shaped by your kind convictions into
disciples whose lives are more streamlined for your service,
and whose joys are more nearly as your own.

Let us better learn this day what it means to travel light through
this short life, holding loosely our material possessions,
storing instead our truer treasures in heaven, and directing
the increase of our devotions more constantly toward you.

Center our hearts again in you, O Lord.
Let us be satisfied in your love.

Amen.

Marking of Birthdays

How marvelous it is, O Lord,
that you contemplated each of us
before we were made!

How marvelous that you considered and created us,
decreeing the very time and place that each of us should enter
the world, to live out our own part of your grand story.
And so we celebrate today the first appearance of
_____ in the epic tale of redemption.

We gather to celebrate, and to give thanks that their
life and days are woven with ours, that we might share
the joys and burdens of life together, delighting in the ways
your glory is reflected in the unrepeatable gift of their being.

You have created each of us, O Lord, to bear your image
in unique expression, reflecting a facet of your glory
in a way that no other person in all of history will,
so that by knowing one another we might also know you better.
And so we celebrate and honor your image, O God, uniquely
reflected in the life and in the personhood of _____.

Bless this your child in the year to come. May they know
the comfort of your presence, the certainty of your purpose,
and the consolation of your love at work in their life.

Grant them
    wisdom,
    maturity,
    vision,
    and passion
in increasing measure, that they might be an instrument
well-honed for the building of your kingdom.

Bless them with loving family and enduring friendships,
that they might make their journey ever surrounded by
the steadying companionship of fellow pilgrims.

May they invest their moments well in the coming year
and in all years to follow, living life always with the end in view,
in pursuit of that eternal prize that will allow them to look
ever with gladness and never with regret upon the passing of
their years, as each subsequent birthday will be but the
marking of a step nearer to the final fulfillment of
all they have so long hoped and labored for.

Amen.

LITURGIES OF
Petition
& Provision

A LITURGY FOR THE
Ritual of Morning Coffee

Meet me, O Christ,
    in this stillness of morning.
Move me, O Spirit,
    to quiet my heart.
Mend me, O Father,
    from yesterday's harms.

From the discords of yesterday,
    resurrect my peace.
From the discouragements of yesterday,
    resurrect my hope.
From the weariness of yesterday,
    resurrect my strength.
From the doubts of yesterday,
    resurrect my faith.
From the wounds of yesterday,
    resurrect my love.

Let me enter this new day, aware of my need,
and awake to your grace, O Lord.

Amen.

A LITURGY FOR A

Sick Day

For this brief pause, for this reminder of my own weakness
and of my dependence upon you, I thank you, O Lord.

A day such as this, in which I endure a measure of sickness
or unease, is a reminder that the redemption of all things
is not yet complete. It is a reminder that this body will decline
and one day fail, and so it is also a reminder that the ways
I spend my days matter—for my hours, revealed like veins
of gold beneath a rushing stream, are a limited resource
to be purposefully mined or forever lost.

A day such as this is a reminder that good health and vigor
are gifts to be consciously and gratefully enjoyed, and to be
invested while they might, in eternal things. So let me finish
this day, O Lord, wiser than I began it.

Let me live now, in light of the knowledge that a time might
come in this life when I feel such sickness and discomfort for
a long season, when I must adjust to a "new normal," when my
abilities are limited either by the slow decline of age or from
some accident, injury, or disease. Therefore let me use the good
health that I have while I have it, presuming nothing.

Let me use it to serve well, to love well,
to care for your people, your creation,
to spend my allotted days
    cherishing hearts,
    creating beauty,
    bringing order,
    offering healing,
delighting in your goodness manifest to me in a
million ways, and so to one day come to the end
of my days having stewarded them well.

Heal my body from this sickness,
O Christ My Healer.
Be gracious. Give rest.

Raise me again to health with a heightened sense
of thankfulness for the unmerited gift of well-being,
and also with a greater sense of compassion for those
who suffer lingering ailment, disease, or discomfort.
Teach me by my own small sufferings to be a better
minister and friend to those who suffer greatly.

So let even the unease I feel today work as your servant,
    accomplishing your better purposes in me.

Amen.

A LITURGY FOR THE
Morning of a Medical Procedure

**INTERCESSORS: You designed our bodies, O Lord,
with a wondrous capacity for regeneration and healing.
You give wisdom and knowledge and skill to those who
by long training in their professions learn to diagnose
and treat ailments of the body. And you, by your Spirit,
sometimes effect miracles of healing that even
the most skilled of practitioners cannot duplicate.**

PATIENT: Today, as I submit myself to this procedure, I ask,
O Lord, that by all means your care toward me would be
manifest, for I am utterly dependent upon you. Give to my
body immunity and vitality that I might recover quickly.
Give me strength and health to resist complications.
Give to my medical providers wisdom, skill, and insight.
And by your Spirit, transcend even what body and medicine
at their best might do. Where it is needed, bring the
healing of your own touch to bear in my mortal frame.

Be merciful, O God.

Show your goodness to me, and to those who share
my concern. Be now my physician, my mender, my healer.
Even in the midst of this procedure, let me rest in you.

Amen.

FOR THOSE FACING INVASIVE, CRITICAL, OR HIGH-RISK
PROCEDURES, AND FOR THOSE FRAUGHT WITH WORRY,
THE FOLLOWING SECTION MAY BE ADDED.

As I approach this procedure I acknowledge my own fears
at the possibility of outcomes I cannot control.

O God unshaken by any circumstance,
be now my rock and my refuge.

Still my racing thoughts.
Speak peace to this gale-storm of my insecurities.
In the midst of my concerns, give me grace to receive
without bitterness the presence and support of friends who,
seeking to ease fears they cannot understand,
might utter unhelpful things.

Give me also grace to trust, to rest my trepidations in you,
for your purposes and your presence transcend
all possible outcomes.

Whether the end result of this procedure brings news
    that is good, bad, or uncertain,
nothing that is essential or eternal will have changed;
My great hope is secure. Let me rest in that.
At the end of this day, I will still be your child,
utterly dependent on you, utterly loved by you.
At the end of this day, my life will yet be hidden with Christ,
even as it now is. I will remain an heir to the promise
that this imperfect, mortal body, though it faces
temporary decline, will one day be swallowed up
in a glorious immortality.

We pray for good outcomes from this procedure, O Lord.
We ask for good outcomes, pleading that you would be
mindful of our mortal frailties,
but we know that regardless of the tidings to come, you are
tender and present and sovereign over all circumstance,
and what is more, you love us fiercely and eternally.

Therefore I would trust you to lead me well along the paths of
any wild and perilous country. You are my shepherd. This day
will hold no surprises for you. Let me rest in that.

Amen.

A LITURGY FOR A HUSBAND & WIFE
At Start of Day

AS ONE: Make of our marriage
a holy habitation, O God.
Ever dwell in us and between us,
teaching us how to be to one another
a truer husband and a truer wife,
your mercy mediating,
your love surrounding,
your Spirit quickening our hearts
unto conviction, repentance, and forgiveness,
unto compassion, kindness, and generosity—
That we would
    in tenderness
seek always to know one another more,
    and in tenderness
allow ourselves to be
more known.

Amen.

A LITURGY FOR A HUSBAND & WIFE
At Close of Day

HUSBAND: At death we will part.
WIFE: **Therefore let us not take for granted**
the blessing of our life together.

SILENCE IS KEPT AS BOTH SPOUSES CONSIDER FOR A
MOMENT THE GRAVITY OF THIS TRUTH.

HUSBAND: May our hearts be ever drawn toward you,
O Lord, in whose three-personed perfection of love burns the
fire that would kindle our two-personed imperfection into
a oneness that is warmed and forged of your holy flames,
WIFE: **a oneness that is both an echo and**
a seed and a play upon a stage, portraying
the promise of union with Christ that is to come.
AS ONE: We are unworthy players, O Lord,
unworthy to portray your glory.

> We are weak.
> We are jealous.
> We are easily wounded.
> We are petty.
> We are embittered.

We store up remembrances of wrongs.
We are insecure.
We hurt one another.
We do not deal with our conflicts well.
We fail to love as you have loved.

Forgive us even the failures of this day.

SILENCE IS KEPT.

IF EITHER HAVE NEED TO MAKE AMENDS, THEY MAY DO SO NOW.

HUSBAND: I am not strong enough
in my own strength to be husband to you.
WIFE: **And I am not strong enough
in my own strength to be wife to you.**
HUSBAND: Let us turn to God together then,
asking the strength that we need.

HUSBAND AND WIFE TAKE HANDS.

AS ONE: Give us therefore the strength that comes from
the grace that flows from your heart alone, O God,
that we might live and move and breathe in the air of
that grace, receiving it in ourselves, and then
offering it daily to one another.

Without grace, our marriage will wither
as a vine unrooted.
But sustained by your grace, it will ever flourish and
bloom and flower and fruit.

HUSBAND: Forgive us our failures and our sins
against one another and against our marriage, O God,
and restore now our hearts to you and to each other.
WIFE: **Repair the damages of our selfishness,
our thoughtlessness, our inconsistencies.
Draw us again together at the close of this day,
in love, and forgiveness, and fellowship, and peace.**
AS ONE: May we sleep this night side by side
in unity of heart and mind and purpose.
May we wake in the morning in solidarity and delight,
thankful for the sharing of this life, for the companion
who journeys beside us, for hands to hold and arms
to embrace, and lips to kiss at the close of day.

HUSBAND: May we love one another more
at the close of this day than we did at its dawning.
WIFE: **May we treasure one another more
at the end of this week than we did at its beginning.**
HUSBAND: May we hold one another as more precious,
more respected, and more dear at the shuttering
of this month, than we did at its opening.

WIFE: **May we delight in our companionship
and take heart in the sharing of our burdens more
at the conclusion of this year, than we did as it began.**

HUSBAND: In the beauty of our bond,
may we reflect your glory more fully in the
hour we are parted by death than we did
in the hour of our wedding.

AS ONE: Bless our marriage. Kindle our desire.
Teach us to be friends and lovers and
companions. May this our marriage exist
not only for our benefit, but may the bond
between us grow to be a shelter and a
blessing for others as well.

HUSBAND: We ask these things in the
name of the Father, and of the Son,
and of the Holy Spirit.
AS ONE: Amen.

HUSBAND: And now, with joined hearts,
WIFE: **we bring to you these burdens of our day.**

HUSBAND AND WIFE MAY NOW FREELY PETITION THEIR
HEAVENLY FATHER WITH ALL WORRIES, BURDENS, AND CONCERNS.

A LITURGY FOR THOSE WHO SUFFER LOSS FROM
Fire, Flood, or Storm

LEADER: O Christ in Whom Our Lives are Hidden,
PEOPLE: **fix now our hope in that which alone might sustain it.**

O Christ in Whom Our Treasures are Secure,
fix now our hope in you.
In light of all that was so suddenly lost, O Lord,
in light of all we had gathered but could not keep,
comfort us.

Our nerves are frayed, O God. Our sense of
place and permanence is shaken,
so be to us a foundation.

We were shaped by this place, and by the living of our lives in it,
by conversations and labors and studies,
by meals prepared and shared, by love incarnated in a
thousand small actions that became as permanent a part of
this structure as any nail or wire or plank of wood.

Our home was to us like a handprint of heaven. It was
our haven, and now we are displaced and faced with
the task of great labors—not to move forward in this life,
but merely to rebuild and restore what has been lost.

Have mercy, Lord Christ.

What we have lost here are the artifacts of our journey
in this world, the very things that reminded us of your grace
expressed in love and friendship, and in shared experience.
**It is for these reasons we grieve the loss of our home and its
contents—we grieve them for what they had come to signify
in our stories, for they were charged with such meaning and
memory, and woven with so much that is eternal.**

O Father, we have suffered a hard loss, and one that we
cannot endure alone. May we emerge in the months to come—
even in our frailty—stronger than before, more deeply rooted
in you, and more wrapped in the necessary arms of community.
Give us humility to receive that which we need and cannot
repay, when it is offered by others.

**We thank you for the presence of friends
who would share this burden of grief
simply by showing up in the midst of it,
and grieving with us.**

We thank you for small mercies and kindnesses extended.
For the grace of thoughtfulness translated into the tiny details
of life. For beauty. O Lord, let us not lose sight in our grief,
of all that is yet bursting with beauty in this world.

**Let us not lose sight of the truth that we live in the midst
of an unfolding story of redemption, and that even this loss
of ours will have its counterpoint at the great restoration.**

Indeed, for anything spared and salvaged, we give you thanks.
Let us see that even in disaster, there is grace still at work,
for you know the limits of our hearts.

**Be with us now as we sift and clean, as we slog merely to
reclaim some fraction of that which we once took for granted.**

Be with us as we navigate the countless details that
must be tended and decisions that must be made
between now and the time that we begin to feel normal again.

**Be with us as we slowly recover from the shock
of sudden loss, enough to begin to imagine what
the restoration of our home might mean,**
for to build again a thing that we know might
easily be lost, must be an act of faith.
**Let our rebuilding be a declaration that a day will come
when all good things are permanent, when disaster and
decay will have no place, when dwellings will stand forever,
and when no more lives will be disrupted by death,
tragedy, reversal, or loss.**

So by that eternal vision, shape our vision for
what this temporary home might become in its repair,
O Lord, that in that process of planning and rebuilding
we might also streamline our lives for stewardship,
for service, and for hospitality in the years ahead.

But those are all tasks for tomorrow.
**We do not even know yet today the full
    measure of what we have lost.**

Today is for mourning. So let us grieve together as those who know
the world is broken, but who yet hold hope of its restoration.

A MOMENT OF SILENCE IS OBSERVED. THEN ANY WHO WISH TO
SPEAK ALOUD THEIR SPECIFIC EXPRESSIONS OF GRIEF MAY DO SO.
THE LEADER THEN CONTINUES WITH THESE WORDS READ BY ALL:

**Comfort us, O Lord, in the wake of what has overtaken us.
Shield us, O Lord, from the hurts we cannot bear.
Shelter us, O Lord, in the fortress of your love.**

Shepherd us, O Lord, as we wake each new morning, faced
with the burdens of a hard pilgrimage we would not have
chosen. But as this is now our path, let us walk it in faith, and
let us walk it bravely, knowing that you go always before us.

Amen.

A LITURGY FOR THE
Loss of Electricity

ONE CANDLE IS LIT, OR ONE FLASHLIGHT SWITCHED ON.

LEADER: O Christ who first spoke light
into darkness, and who, in later days,
came to dwell among us as
the light of the world,
PEOPLE: **be to us now that true light.**

ADDITIONAL CANDLES ARE LIT OR FLASHLIGHTS SWITCHED ON,
IF NEEDED FOR READING.

Be to us that true light even as we pause here in this
sudden and unexpected darkness.

**Shape our hearts, O Spirit of God, as we pause in this
brief absence of blessings so often taken for granted—**
blessings of illumination, of lamps and lights,
of refrigeration, of appliances and digital devices,
of climate control and hot water.

**We thank you for these many comforts
and conveniences we enjoy.**

For you, O Lord, imagined and designed the very physics by
which electrons flow and by which their currents might be
harnessed and channeled toward these useful ends.

You are the King of all creation.

You created the chemistry and the physics of all power sources,
that they might be useful tools when humanely plied,
making labor more fruitful, abating the toil and misery of
many, establishing greater margins for rest and relationship,
and making possible the flourishing of peoples and cultures.

Glory to you, Lord Christ.
We praise you for these hidden mercies.
We praise you even as we pray you would cultivate in us
a vigilant thankfulness, that these comforts we enjoy would
never numb us to our deep need for you.

In love, deliver us from all delusions
of self-sufficiency, O Lord.

Use even little deprivations, like this loss of power, to
reorient our hearts to the all-sufficient Christ, reminding us
that we are not dependent upon comforts or conveniences
for anything that truly matters.
You are our everything, Lord Jesus.

You are with us in times of plenty and in times of want.
You are with us in seasons of comfort
    and in seasons of discomfort.
You are with us in ease and in hardship as well.
You are as present with us in darkness as you are in light.
You are near to us when the electricity is on and when it is off.

So make of us a pilgrim people whose hearts are freed to
face, with joy intact, any deprivation along this journey,
confident that even in losing all comforts we still have you,
confident that in losing all things we have lost nothing
of eternal value, for all our treasures are hid
and guarded in you.

We thank you for this moment without electricity—
a moment in which to remember that all blessings are gifts,
that all good things are expressions of grace, and that you,
no matter our circumstances, are with us always, and will
never leave us or forsake us.

Even now, O Lord, shine into our darkness.
Even now, O Spirit, lead us into that light.
Even now, O Father, let your love illuminate our lives.
Let it be our bright and guiding beacon.
Let it be the lamp of our eternal joy.

Amen.

A LITURGY BEFORE
Serving Others

O Christ Who Made Himself the Servant of All,
I would set my heart and my affections upon you—
and upon you alone—for I can only
serve others rightly when such service
is undertaken from first to last as
an act of devotion offered to you.

In serving you, I am freed from my need for the praise
of others. So that even if my kindnesses are shed from
scarred hearts as rain from a sloped tin roof,
my joy will not be dimmed, for I will know that you
have received and remembered each act of sacrifice,
and reckoned it as a love rendered to you.

So let my love be sincere, and let my service be fearless, O Lord.

I would serve in imitation of you, who poured out your life
for me. I would serve knowing that your Spirit is ever at work
in the lives of those I serve, ever calling, ever drawing,
ever seeking to soften hearts encased in fear and
disappointment and anger and idolatry. So let my kindnesses
and sacrifice fall like warm shafts of sunlight on icy ground.

I cannot know the end of another person's story.
Our lives so often only briefly intersect. So let me
be content to minister regardless
of visible outcomes, trusting that the small mercies
I extend will be woven into the larger theme of
redemption at work in the lives of others as you
woo them to yourself, drawing their hearts
by graces offered, and shaping my own heart too
in this process of learning to serve well, and
by learning to serve well, learning to love well.

Amen.

A LITURGY BEFORE
A Meal Eaten Alone

You created us for companionship, O God,
    for the sharing of burdens,
    for the joining of celebrations,
    for the breaking of bread in fellowship,
and so it is not unnatural that we should taste
a particular sorrow when eating a meal alone.

Sit with me and linger at this solitary table, O Lord.

Sit with me as my father.
Sit with me as my brother.
Sit with me as my shepherd.
Sit with me as my friend.
In the absence of human companions,
may I know more fully your presence.
In this silence where there is no conversation,
may I more clearly hear your voice.

Use my own momentary loneliness
to work in me a more effectual sympathy
for others who are often alone,
and who long for the companionship
of their God and of his people.

Let me afterward be more intentional
in the practice of hospitality.
Let me sometimes be the reason
the loneliness of another is relieved.
Meet me now in my own loneliness, O Lord.
Meet me in this meal. I receive it as your
provision for my life in this hour.

Amen.

A LITURGY FOR THOSE FLOODED BY
Too Much Information

In a world so wired and interconnected,
our anxious hearts are pummeled by an endless barrage of troubling news. We are daily aware of more grief, O Lord,
than we can rightly consider, of more suffering and scandal
than we can respond to, of more hostility, hatred, horror,
and injustice than we can engage with compassion.

But you, O Jesus, are not disquieted by such news of cruelty
and terror and war. You are neither anxious nor overwhelmed.
You carried the full weight of the suffering of a broken world
when you hung upon the cross, and you carry it still.

When the cacophony of universal distress unsettles us, remind
us that we are but small and finite creatures, never designed
to carry the vast abstractions of great burdens, for
our arms are too short and our strength is too small.
  Justice and mercy, healing and redemption,
   are your great labors.

And yes, it is your good pleasure to accomplish such works
through your people, but you have never asked any one of us
to undertake more than your grace will enable us to fulfill.

Guard us then from shutting down our empathy or
walling off our hearts because of the glut of unactionable
misery that floods our awareness. You have many children
in many places around this globe. Move each of our hearts
to compassionately respond to those needs that intersect
our actual lives, that in all places your body might be actively
addressing the pain and brokenness of this world, each of us
liberated and empowered by your Spirit to fulfill the
small part of your redemptive work assigned to us.

Give us discernment
     in the face of troubling news reports.
Give us discernment
     to know when to pray, when to speak out,
     when to act, and when to simply shut off
     our screens and our devices,
     and to sit quietly
     in your presence,

casting the burdens of this world
upon the strong shoulders
of the one who
     alone
is able to bear them up.

Amen.

A LITURGY FOR THOSE WHO COVET
The Latest Technology

Content my soul in you, O Christ,
who alone are sufficient to my longings.

When my heart is beset by wheedling desire
for what it does not have,
remind me, sweet Jesus, that I have no right
to a thing, simply because it exists.
The perpetual allure of new innovation
does not negate the call to faithfully steward
those resources you have temporarily
entrusted to my keeping.

Guard my heart therefore against idols
of silicon and circuitry enticing
with slick-veneered promises of
a more sophisticated and upgraded lifestyle.

Content my soul in you, O Christ,
who alone are sufficient to my longings.
In such moments of technological temptation,
when I might justify to myself the reasonableness
of a costly purchase, speak louder, O Lord,

than the voice of my self-serving thoughts.
If there is no real need for, or true wisdom in,
the purchase of a new technology, service, or application,
then let me be content with fewer options,

>   slower speeds, smaller memory,
>   less diversion, less gadgetry.

Let me be content, O Lord, with what I truly need
to accomplish the necessary tasks before me.

Nay, let me be content with nothing but thee.
O Christ who alone art sufficient to my longings,

>   I would be your trusted servant,
>   at liberty to employ and to enjoy all things at my disposal,
>   without being owned by any of them—
>   using technologies to further good ends,
>   while never seeking them as ends in themselves.
>   For it is not the advance of digital platforms
>   that will usher in your kingdom,
>   but the work of your Spirit in the world,
>   and in the hearts and lives of your people.

Content my soul therefore in you, O Christ,
who alone are sufficient to my longings.

Amen.

A LITURGY FOR ONE

Battling a Destructive Desire

Jesus, here I am again,
    desiring a thing
    that were I to indulge in it
    would war against my own heart,
    and the hearts of those I love.

O Christ, rather let my life be thine!
Take my desires. Let them be subsumed
in still greater desire for you,
until there remains no room
    for these lesser cravings.

In this moment I might choose
to indulge a fleeting hunger,
or I might choose
to love you more.

Faced with this temptation,
I would rather choose you, Jesus—
but I am weak. So be my strength.
I am shadowed. Be my light.
I am selfish. Unmake me now,

and refashion my desires
according to the better designs of your love.

Given the choice of shame or glory,
    let me choose glory.
Given the choice of this moment or eternity,
    let me choose in this moment what is eternal.
Given the choice of this easy pleasure,
or the harder road of the cross,
    give me grace to choose to follow you,
    knowing that there is nowhere apart from your
    presence where I might find the peace I long for,
    no lasting satisfaction apart from your
    reclamation of my heart.

Let me build, then, my King,
a beautiful thing by long obedience,
by the steady progression of small choices
that laid end to end will become like the stones
of a pleasing path stretching to eternity and
unto your welcoming arms and unto the sound
of your voice pronouncing the judgment:

   Well done.

A LITURGY FOR
Nights & Days of Doubt

I would that my heart was ever strong, O Lord,
    my faith always firm and unwavering,
    my thoughts unclouded,
    my devotion sincere,
    my vision clear.

I would that I dwelt always in that state wherein my belief,
my hope, my confidence, were rooted and certain.

I would that I could remain in those seasons
when assailing storms seem only to make faith stronger,
proving your presence, your providence.

But it is not always so.

There are those other moments, as now, when
I cannot sense you near, cannot hear you, see you,
touch you—times when fear or depression or frustration
overwhelm, and I find no help or consolation, when
the seawalls of my faith crumble and give way to
inrushing tides of doubt.

Have I believed in vain?
Are your words true?
    They seem so distant to me now.
Is your presence real?
    I cannot feel it.
Do you love me?
    Or are you indifferent to my grief?
Under weight of such darkness, how can I remember the
sunlight of your love as anything more than a child's dream?
Under weight of such doubt, how can I still proclaim
to my own heart with certainty that you are real?

And so, Jesus, I do now the only thing I know to do.

Here I drag my heavy heart again into this cleared and desolate
space, to see if you will meet me in my place of doubt, even as
you mercifully met your servant Thomas in his uncertainty,
even as you once acted in compassionate response to a fearful
father who desperately pleaded:

   I believe, Lord. Help me with my unbelief!

For where else but to you might I flee with my doubts?
You alone have the words of eternal life.

A LONG SILENCE IS KEPT.

This I know to be true, my Lord and my God:
You are not in the least angered by my doubts and
my questions, for they have often been the very things
that lead me to press closer in to you,
seeking the comfort of your presence,
seeking to understand the roots of my own confusion.

So also use these present doubts for your purposes, O Lord.
I offer them to you. Even as the patriarch Job made of his pain
and confusion a petition; even as the psalmists again and again
carried their cries, their questions, their laments to you;
so would I be driven by my doubts to despair of my own
strength and knowledge and righteousness and control,
and instead to seek your face, knowing that when I plead
for proof, what I most need is your presence.

In your presence I can offer my questions,
knowing you are never threatened by my uncertainties.
They do not change your truth.
My doubts cannot unseat your promises.
You are a rock, O Christ,
and your truth is a bulwark
that I might dash myself against,
until my strength is spent
and I collapse at last in despair,

only then to feel the tenderness of
your embrace as you stoop to gather me to yourself,
drawing me to your breast and cradling me there,
where I find I am held again by a love that
even my doubts cannot undo.

O Lord, how many times have you graciously led me
through doubt into a deeper faith?
    Do so again, my Lord and my God!
    Even now. Do so again!

You alone are strong enough
to carry the weight of my troubled thoughts,
    even as you alone are strong enough
    to bear the burden of my sin and my guilt and
    my shame, my wounds and my brokenness.

O Christ, let my doubts never compel me
to hide my heart from you.
Let them rather arise as questions
to begin holy conversations.
Invert these doubts,
turning them to invitations to be present,
    to be honest,
    to seek you,
    to cry out to you,

    to bring my heart fully into the struggle
rather than to seek to numb it.

Let my doubts become invitations to wrestle
with you through such dark nights of the soul
—as Jacob wrestled with the Angel
—until the day breaks anew
and I am fresh wounded by your love
and resting in the blessing of peace
    again in your presence.

Now O Lord may the end result of my doubt be
a more precious and hard-wrung faith,
resilient as the Methuselah tree, and
a hope more present and evergreen, and
a more tender and active mercy extended to others
in their own seasons of doubting.

So help me,
    my Lord and my God.
I have no consolation but you.
Meet me now in this eclipse-shadow of my doubt.

Lead me again into your light.

Amen.

A LITURGY FOR THOSE WITH
A Sudden Burden to Intercede

I sense your beckoning, O Lord, and I willingly respond,
entering your presence to plead on behalf of another.
Spirit of God, you alone know the specific needs of
the one for whom I am suddenly burdened to intercede.

Therefore guide my prayer.

Tune my thoughts, my words, my empathies
to articulate your greater heart,
your deeper purposes.
I yield to your intentions,
even unto the breaking of my own heart
for that which breaks yours.

Through me, O God, may it please you to bring forth
effective petition for the one whose condition has
so moved your heart that you have now moved mine, calling
me to fervent prayer—

    to cry out,
    to contend,
    to do battle—
on their behalf.

Breathe through me, O Spirit,
your thoughts, your words.
Kindle in me, O Father,
your sorrows and consolations.
Teach me, O Christ, how to serve
and to love by intercession.

**SILENCE IS KEPT, FOR THE CENTERING OF THE HEART AND THE
SENSING OF THE SPIRIT'S PROMPTINGS IN PRAYER. NOW MAKE
PETITION AND INTERCESSION ON BEHALF OF THOSE YOU ARE
BURDENED FOR.**

Intersect our moments with your mercies, O Lord.
Intersect our days with evidence of your grace.
Let this burden remain or return as often
as you would have me carry it again to you.

You are ever at work in this world. So let
my compassion be always active and
my heart sensitive to your movements,
your promptings, your revelation.

Call us, your children, always to care for one another
in prayer and in action, in our various times of need.

Amen.

A LITURGY FOR THOSE WHO FEEL
Awkward in Social Gatherings

I know this about myself, O Lord:
> You have created me
> as one who best flourishes
> with daily rhythms of solace
> and long moments
> for quiet reflection.

When I find myself instead
in noisy, crowded spaces
amidst constant social interactions,
my energies are soon depleted,
and I am left feeling inadequate,
awkward, uncomfortable.

I know this about myself, O Lord:
> In a room full of people,
> I would rather retreat into a quiet corner
> and flip through the pages of a book
> than step beyond the walls of my self
> to engage another person in conversation.

And this desire, in and of itself,
is neither a sin nor a virtue, but simply

a description of my feelings—and yet
it presents me with a choice.

For you have not called me to insulate my heart from others,
or from the discomfort I might feel in the
presence of acquaintances and strangers.

You have called me instead to learn to love
by my small actions and choices,
those whose paths I cross,
moment to moment, in all settings.

And so, despite my shyness,
I would rather learn to emulate your mercies
by entering the lives of others,
affirming their dignity and worth simply
by showing interest in the details of their lives,
however awkward I might feel in the process.

Give me grace therefore, O God, to love others,
to move toward them when my instinct is to run.

Here is my social clumsiness, my insecurity, my weariness,
my fear of rejection. And here also is my desire to be
your emissary and your child.
Use them as you will.

You do not call me to be cool, to be sophisticated, to be
    charming, to be the life of the party.
You do not call me to be a social butterfly or to
    work the room.
You call me simply to love,
    even in my own bumbling way.
Somehow use my very weakness, O God,
    in the service of your kingdom.

When next I find myself in a room filled with people, where
the din of conversation is disorienting, do what I cannot:
Quell my discomfort enough
that I might consider with true compassion
the needs of another human being.
Then let me consciously,
    and as an act of love and choosing to love,
move toward that person.
Let your grace compel my movements.
In such moments, let me think less of myself
    and my own awkwardness.
Let me think more of others.

In all moments, let me think less of myself
and my own awkwardness, O Lord,

and let me think more of you.

A LITURGY FOR
Dating or Courtship

Here is where I am, O Lord—

I find myself drawn to one in whom I see
a striking beauty of personhood,
a depth of soul,
a sensitivity to goodness and truth,
a vibrant intentionality of life and choice.

I praise you, God, for creating such a person and
displaying in them unique expression
of your glory.

I thank you that my path has crossed theirs
in this time and place in history.
I am increasingly drawn to this one you have
created, and I desire to know them more.
But I am finite and limited,
and I cannot see the path that lies ahead
on this journey toward eternity.
    So give me wisdom, Lord.
    Do not let my emotions get ahead of me.

In the time that I spend with this your beloved
child, let me not act selfishly. Let me not take
lightly my constant responsibility for the heart
and well-being of another, regardless of the
tenor of my own feelings and desires.

Let me remember that this relationship
does not affect only the two of us.
It exists in that greater web of loving and
sacrificial bonds of parents and grandparents,
family and friends, who had already invested
years of nurture and care and love and prayer
and tears and delight in this person,
long before I ever met them.

So let me act now, and always in this relationship,
in ways that would honor and affirm
the tender investment of all who love this person.
Let me build on that good foundation, that
whatever the two of us create together
would be a blessing to all who know us.

Indeed, O Lord, give us in our shared hours wisdom
to build well, that even if all we cultivate in partnership
is a small garden where friendship can grow,
it will still in its own humble way be a place

of encouragement and beauty that would
bring a smile and a joy to passers-by.

Or if we awaken one day to the understanding
that what we were creating all along was
not just a garden of friendship, but an
enduring love, and the foundations of a castle, and
a tended ground where the remainder of our lives and
the lives of our children and grandchildren and
all of our friendships and all of our service to you,
O God, would be lived out together in a bond of
wedded love and intimacy, then all the more reason
we should build well and with intentionality and
unselfish love here at the beginning.

Give me this wisdom, therefore.
Give me this grace.
Give me patience and an eternal perspective that would govern
well my choices today, and in all the days to follow.

Do not let my emotions get ahead of me, O Lord.
Let me love you by loving this person well, and in kindness
and self-restraint let me always choose their greatest good
     as if it were my own.

Amen.

A LITURGY BEFORE
Giving I

In truth, I have nothing but you, O Christ,
nothing that I might call my own.

So let that good confession now
compel a better stewardship.

First teach me to treasure
you, Jesus, above all things. Then
let that increasing devotion be
increasingly demonstrated in a joyful
generosity—for to give is to live out
the declaration that you alone are
my provision and supply. I need
not fear what comes tomorrow.

When I give to meet the needs of others,
when I give to the work of those who serve the poor,
the sick, the oppressed, when I give to the service of
your Body and your Kingdom, I give not what is mine,
but only what is already yours. With every charitable act
I am simply practicing the fact that nothing which passes
through my hands has ever belonged to me.

You are my generous master.
Make me your faithful trustee, teaching me
to live as a wiser conduit of this liberal grace,
learning to hold loosely the things of this world,
never hoarding that which is yours, never seeking
the mean preservation of my own comforts. Rather
let me love well in my giving, even as you,
O Father, have loved me so well by
giving me all things in Christ.

Let me make each offering without thought of temporal gain.
Let me give precisely because I have believed your promises
are true—and let my giving be the proof. If you are my
shepherd, then I am freed to live generously, knowing
I will never want for any needful thing—knowing that any
seeming deprivation is but the work of your Spirit
weaning me from a world of things and winning me to
greater dependence upon Christ my King.

So why should I grasp at that which I cannot keep?
This body will sleep in death and what I now hold
so briefly will pass into the keeping of another.
I own nothing here. I have no claim.
Dispel the myth of my possessions,
lest they taint that better hope of Heaven.

Rather let me learn, while I draw breath,
to live with open hands and joy-filled heart,
investing your resources in your good works.
Let me plant these mortal seeds
in expectation of immortal harvests.

**THE FINAL SECTION MAY BE USED AS STAND-ALONE VERSION OF THE
LITURGY.**

Bless now, O Lord, this gift and its benefits, that
it might be received as evidence of your mercies, and
multiplied in effectiveness for your kingdom.
Through this and other acts of giving,
train my heart toward a greater generosity, that
the habits of my stewardship might be
ever more pleasing to you, and
ever more expressive of your own
holy heart and passions.

    All that I have is yours, Lord Christ.
    All that I have is you.

Use then this small gift for works of love and mercy,
and unto the increase of your glory.

Amen.

A LITURGY BEFORE
Giving II

Ah Lord, let that best love which shapes my life
    be evident even in my accountings.

Let that which I most treasure
be revealed in long columns
of expenditures that
month to month and year to year accrue
like the clues of a treasure map, revealing
where my heart and my hope are hidden.

Let me learn to love you by this glad practice of giving,
taking joy in every opportunity to invest in that
heavenly economy whose scale of return will
prove to be so out of proportion to all
earthly paradigms as to render them
at last trivial and absurd.

Let me give—neither as begrudging duty nor from some
blasphemous belief that you might be manipulated—
but let me give in sincerity and cheerfulness, as
a means of making evident the infinite implications of
the gospel. Let me give to that which moves your heart.

Let me give
    to give food to the hungry,
    water to the thirsty,
    shelter to the homeless,
    relief to the refugee,
    aid to the orphan,
    freedom to the captive,
    justice to the oppressed,
    mercy to the broken,
    good news to the poor,
    healing to the sick,
    comfort to the distressed,
    consolation to the lonely,
    sight to the blind,
    hope to the hopeless,
    peace to the war-weary,
    reconciliation to those in conflict,
    and the liberating story of your love
        to those who hunger for it.

Ah Lord, let that best love
which shapes my life
be evident in this and in all my
small acts of giving.

Amen.

A LITURGY FOR THOSE WITH AN
Impulse to Buy

I know, O Lord, that you are no petty tyrant,
begrudging your creatures every passing happiness.
You have crafted a creation fraught with small pleasures,
and have fashioned us with great capacity to
enjoy pleasurable things.

So it is not from a sense of dour asceticism
that I pause to question my desire to
purchase a thing I suddenly want. It is,
rather, because I have ample reason
not to trust my reasons for wanting.

In hindsight I see how the history of my stewardship
is spotted with the acquisition of costly things
I might in sober judgment have foregone—

Things I have not used enough to justify their cost,
things I could not well afford,
things that actively warred
against wise use of my time,
luxuries that offered no true benefit, things
purchased on impulse when a more reasoned and

prayerful consideration might have led me
to a better stewardship of your trust, O God.

So sensing now some warning sign embedded
in this new desire to buy, I would first pause,
asking that I might—
under your Spirit's right conviction—
better divine my own motives unto
the end that I might be wiser in my choosing.

If the dissonance I sense is a holy constraint,
then increase that inhibition. Give me restraint
to wait at least until that first, powerful impulse
passes, that I might make sound consideration.

Whether this purchase might in the end be wise
or no, I would still wrestle well with the question,
and so learn by practice to hobble my old habit
of purchasing on flimsy whims.

This is hardly about the purchase of
a thing anyway,
is it, O God?

It is mostly about my heart,
and what I treasure, and where I seek my satisfaction.

So let me learn to love you enough, O Lord, that
I need no constant stream of bright and shiny things
to ease some itch or ache within my soul.
Free my heart from craven clenching, as if
ownership of a thing could ever bring about
       the gain of anything eternal.

I know I cannot keep the things I hold, and so
I would not sleepwalk through this life,
always amassing that which will be of no true benefit.

Let me instead, O Lord, tend well what you have trusted to my
keeping, planting good seed for future reaping in eternal fields.
Yes, I would enjoy the pleasures you place in my life, and
I would let such enjoyments always turn my heart again in
praise to you for your many blessings. But I do not want
to seek such pleasures at the expense of good stewardship,
or allow them any pilfered share of my heart's devotion.

So teach me in this moment, O God,
how to yield my small desires to your greater will.
Give me wisdom for the making of sound decisions.
Let me learn by practice what it means to
seek first your kingdom, your purposes, your glory.

Amen.

A LITURGY BEFORE
Shopping

You created us as embodied beings, O Lord
and placed us within a physical creation,
declaring it a good thing. Therefore
it is without shame that we acknowledge our need
of food and shelter and clothing, for it is those same
needs that teach us ever to look to you for our provision.

You created us also as souled creatures,
hungry for knowledge and beauty, nurtured by
music and story and artistry, informed by the
act of creating. You designed us, body and soul,
with inbuilt need for work and for rest, for
fellowship and for play—and the meeting of
each of these diverse needs requires, at times,
the purchase of goods and services.

Therefore, before we venture this day to shop, seeking
things necessary for the care of body and soul,
center our hearts again in the knowledge of who you are,
and of who we are in you, that we might engage in our
commerce, not as unquestioning consumers, but as conscious
curators of your blessings, for ever since that tragedy in Eden,

our relationship to *things* has been upended.
Shame, insecurity, fear, envy, vanity, and pride now
threaten to nudge us from a right posture of
grateful stewardship. Constant calls to consume
surround and assail us, proclaiming that with one purchase

 we might be perceived as more successful,

 more fashionable, more desirable, more cool—
until even our right longings for affirmation and love are
leveraged against us, skewing our desires so that
we mistake wants for needs and are tempted to define ourselves
not by our adoption as your sons and daughters, but by the
shallowest measures of what we have and wear and drive.

Root us rather in you, O Christ,
that we would not fall prey to such false witnesses
playing upon our fears—to the blare and glare of ads and
images that fail to account for the existence of the soul or
for the deepest needs of creatures

 created to inhabit eternity.

Spare us the heartbreak, O Lord, of trusting in things
 that cannot hold the weight of our greatest hopes.
Spare us the heartbreak, O Lord, of chasing after things
 that cannot bear the burden of our greatest sorrows.

As our hearts will be most fixed on what we
most treasure, kindle instead our love for you
ere we set foot in stores or shop online.
For if we love you best, our spending of money
will become a natural expression of our best love,
and a welcome opportunity to learn
and to practice our faithfulness.

Give us grace therefore to accept with grateful thanks that
which we are given. Teach us the difference
between appreciation and idolatry,
between holy enjoyment and wanton indulgence,
between thanksgiving for your provision
and misuse of the resources with which
you have entrusted us.

Tune our consciences till they thrum to the resonant tones
of your Spirit. Teach us contentment. Teach us generosity.
Let us delight in giving to others as you
have delighted in giving to us.

THE CLOSING SECTION MAY ALSO BE USED INDEPENDENTLY
AS AN ABBREVIATED "LITURGY BEFORE SHOPPING"
IF TIME OR CIRCUMSTANCES ARE NOT CONDUCIVE
TO USE OF THE FULL LITURGY.

Be ever at work in our minds and hearts,
O Lord, freeing us from a service to things
by daily increasing our devotion to you.
Liberate us now and always to live as
ever wiser and more compassionate
administrators of the trust and resources you have
placed in our temporary keeping.

May our purchases,
    and our decisions not to purchase,
each be made in the same context
of delighting in your blessings,
of stewarding such gifts in the bright hope
of one day hearing you pronounce over our lives
that most coveted verdict:

Well done, good and faithful servant!
You have been faithful with a few things;
I will put you in charge of many things.
Come and share your master's happiness!

Let the hope of that good end, O Lord,
shape our vision and our choices as we shop today.

Amen.

A LITURGY FOR THE
Paying of the Bills

LEADER: O God Who Does Provide
    All Things Necessary for Our Lives,
PEOPLE: **Be present with us now, in the paying of these bills.**

For there is little in this life that will so starkly reveal
our insecurities and our struggle to trust your tender care
as will the state of our hearts when we consider
the state of our finances—
When we are anxious about money, O Lord,
we can slip so easily into the downward spiral of believing
that simply having more of it would guarantee our security.

As if our security could ever rest anywhere outside of you, O God.
So guard our hearts against that lie.
Let us learn to view money and all material things as an arena
in which to learn and practice a more faithful stewardship,
and as a means by which to invest in things eternal—
but never as ends in themselves.

Where we have mismanaged your provision,
where we have stumbled in our stewardship and
our undoing has been our own doing,

where we have through the workings of our own desires
unwisely accrued expenses or debt,
grant us conviction, and vision, and better wisdom,
that we would more faithfully steward
these resources in months to come.
But where we are merely beset by the common and
inescapable expenses of faithfully tending the many needs
within our spheres of responsibility,
give us peace and, O Lord, give us even joy, to see as we
allocate these funds for the paying of necessary bills, how you
have faithfully provided the means by which to pay them.
And if we have enough to do that, let us practice
contentment in what you have provided.

And if we have more than enough to do that, then teach
us what it would mean to begin to live more generously
towards those whose needs are greater than our own.
For we have you, and in having you we have all things,
and month-to-month you are teaching us—
in this paying of bills—the slow vocation of trust.
Do not abandon us to our anxieties over finances, O Lord,
but use those worries to turn our hearts and thoughts to you—
then teach us both a greater contentment
and a greater confidence in your constant care.

Amen.

A LITURGY FOR ONE WHO HAS
Suffered a Nightmare

I have awakened afraid,
    in need of your comfort, O God.
I have awakened in darkness,
    in need of your light.

    Father, keep watch.
    Spirit, calm fear.
    Jesus, be near.

Your presence abides with your children forever,
and I am your child. Therefore, I know that you are with me.

    I am not alone.
    I am never alone.
    You are here.

    Father, keep watch.
    Spirit, calm fear.
    Jesus, be near.

Kindle in my heart the fires of holy affection,
casting out all disturbing shadows.

Bless the remainder of this night with healing rest.
Comfort me with the knowledge that you do not slumber.
Console me with the promise that your presence is
a constant covering, enfolding me more closely
    than even the blankets of my bed.

Let me draw courage from your fierce and unyielding love,
even in moments when I am afraid.

    Father, keep watch.
    Spirit, speak peace.
    Jesus, draw near even now as I sleep.

Amen.

A LITURGY FOR THOSE WHO
Cannot Sleep

O Christ Who Is My Rest,
This tension of body, and racing of mind, and clamoring of heart
afford me no peace in this night.

Unable to sleep I would yet make use
    of my restlessness, O Lord.

Amidst doubt, anxiety, uncertainty, I would
learn to practice a more constant awareness of
your presence, directing heart and
thought and petition to you.

**HERE THE PERSON MAY UNBURDEN THEIR HEART IN CONVERSATION WITH
GOD, BRINGING TO HIM ANY SPECIFIC ANXIETIES AND CONCERNS.**

Lay your hand upon my brow, O Lord,
and bid me calm. I cannot know every
reason why sleep so evades me, and yet
you have made me yours and in
that knowledge I would know comfort
as a child cradled in a mother's arms,
who sleeping or waking cares not
for which momentary state, but only for
that sweet, unspoken communion of
knowing they are held in the soothing strength
of a great love that is their precious nurture
and their perfect peace.

So even in haggard sleeplessness,
I would yet recognize my utter dependence
upon you, remembering that you are with me
        whether I sleep or not.

I do pray that sleep will come.
I pray that a blessed calm will descend.
I pray that peace will rest upon me now,
that my brow will soon smooth in slumber.
But even if it will not—even if mind or body
refuse their rest—still let my soul take its repose
in the enfolding comfort of your presence,
my head reclined against your breast, hearing
the deep music of your heartbeat.

Waking or sleeping, O Lord,
    be this night my rest,
    and on the morrow, my strength.

Amen.

A LITURGY FOR
First Waking

I am not the captain of my own destiny,
nor even of this new day, and so
I renounce anew all claim
to my own life and desires.
I am only yours, O Lord.

Lead me by your mercies through these hours,
that I might spend them well,
not in harried pursuit of my own agendas, but
rather in good service to you.

Teach me to shepherd the small duties
of this day with great love,
tending faithfully those tasks
you place within my care
and tending with patience and
kindness the needs and hearts of
those people you place within my reach.

Nothing is too hard for you, Lord Christ.
I deposit now all confidence in you
that whatever these waking hours bring,
my foundations will not be shaken.

At day's end I will lay me down again to sleep
knowing that my best hope is well kept in you.

In all things your grace will sustain me.
    Bid me follow,
    and I will follow.

Amen.

LITURGIES OF
Sorrow
& Lament

A LITURGY FOR THOSE WHO HAVE
Not Done Great Things for God

IN 3 PARTS, FOR PETITIONER & INTERCESSOR
PART I: FOR THE PETITIONER

How many times have I been told,
O Christ, by well-meaning people,
that it is my destiny and my charge
to go out into the world
and do great things for you?

How many times in response have
I prayed earnestly, asking that you
would bring such things to pass—
that you might use me mightily
for the work of your kingdom?
How many times have I then waited expectantly.
     And waited.
     And waited
for that great thing, whatever it might be,
to be made obvious?

How many times have I felt then
the gradually settling weight of disillusionment,
of disappointment and confusion,

when no *great thing* materialized, when no
life-changing opportunity suddenly
arrived at my doorstep, when no such moment
of call or clarity was ever manifest at all?

In the confused afterglow of those receding anticipations,
I am always faced again with the unglamorous reality of
my own life:
    of my ongoing failures simply to love well
    the people around me, and of
    my own everpresent struggle
    even to desire and to pursue
    a path of righteousness
    and obedience in my own
    small daily choices and habits.
I am faced again with the same litany of tired,
old temptations towing their attendant shames,
and in such times I am left, O Lord,
wondering if I have somehow missed
your call completely, and whether I might
just as well abandon this pilgrim path entirely,
for I fear that you must see me as I see myself:
    unfit
for any service to you,
or to your people,
or to this world.

So tell me, my God, where is the disconnect
between that life rife with breathtaking
demonstrations of your power
that I am told should be the hallmark
of my walk with you—
where is the disconnect between
those fantastic notions and the reality
of my actual life, which is filled with petty
frustrations, mundane responsibilities,
and constant reminders of my own failure
to wear well the name of Christ?

Was it wrong that I should even desire
to do great things for you, Jesus?
Am I amiss to plead that I might be mightily
used in your works?
    Do I need more faith?
    More righteousness?
    More of your Spirit?
Or have you simply judged me unworthy of your service?
Where, O Lord, do I go from here?

A MOMENT OF SILENCE IS KEPT,

FOR THIS IS A GRIEF THAT, ONCE EXPRESSED,

SHOULD BE ALLOWED TO FINISH ITS HOLLOWING WORK.

PART II: FOR THE INTERCESSOR

(THE PART OF **INTERCESSOR** MIGHT BE READ BY ANY WHO ARE OF
THE PRIESTHOOD OF BELIEVERS—WHICH IS THE BODY OF CHRIST.)

O Child of God, listen well, and be comforted.
He has never judged you unfit for any service
he has called you to,
for it is in Christ's righteousness he has clothed you.
And his measure of greatness has never been your own.
If you would pray to do great things for your God,
then you must pray such prayers without regard
for how they should be answered.

Pray them knowing that
in his true and holy reckoning
such greatness will most often be expressed
in a long practice of humble and sacrificial servanthood,
    and not in any pursuit
    promising a rise to power, position, or prestige.
His might is most often displayed as the grace that cradles
and transcends our brokenness and poverty of spirit.
If you would be so broken, that the light of his grace
might be more visible within you,
shining from your chipped seams and shattered fragments,
then by all means make such earnest requests of him;
make them with sincerity and without reservation!

But if the root of your prayer is rather some desire
for a heightened prominence or sense of accomplishment
and worth—either in your own eyes or in the eyes of others
—then it would be better not to pray such prayers at all.
Examine well your heart and motives,
before asking that his greatness be displayed in your life.
When he answers, it will not be on your terms.

For it is not you that will do any great thing for God, but
God laboring in you and through you who will
greatly accomplish his own good purposes according to
the workings of his sovereignty and love.

Be liberated now from this burden of believing that
anything depends upon you—and so be liberated at last
to give yourself to his joyful service in grateful response
for the grace he has lavished upon you!

You have till now been too invested in the results of
your own efforts, as if those outcomes were a thing
you could ever know or measure in this life!

Be invested instead, child, in simple obedience to your king,
and in long faithfulness to his call, shepherding daily
those gifts and tasks and relationships he has entrusted
to you, regardless of outcomes and appearances.

He will bring all things right in his way and in his time.
All he asks is your willingness.

> Your heart is in his hands.
> Your ways are in his hands.
> Your days are in his hands.

Be content in the station he has appointed you to in
this season, and yet be ever ready to move at the
impulse of his love. Tend well those things
that are before you, however humble they be, and
he will lead you in time to other good works
he has appointed for you.
Whether big or small is of no matter.
He attaches no numbers to your service.
It is your heart and faithfulness he appraises.

Seek not your own glory. Seek God, and his glory will be
seen in you, radiant in humility and in the strength of
his might made manifest even in your brokenness,
evident even in the smallest of services rendered unto him or
offered in his name, even though they be seen by none but
you and him; your reward is secure.

**THE INTERCESSOR NOW CUPS THE HAND OF THE PETITIONER IN
HIS OR HER OWN AND PRAYS SILENTLY FOR THEM A MOMENT.**

PART III: FOR PETITIONER & INTERCESSOR TOGETHER

INTERCESSOR: Is this still your heart's true desire then,
to do great works for the kingdom of heaven?
PETITIONER: It is, though I had not known before
even what it meant. I ask now for grace that I might truly
and humbly repent of any root of vainglory buried in my
former prayers, and I pray also for grace that I might now ask
aright, in purity of heart, that the good works of God would be
manifest in their many outworkings in my heart and life,
at all times and in all endeavors, howsoever it pleases him.
INTERCESSOR: Amen.
Now, child of God, avail yourself of his Spirit, that you might
go and learn to love God and love others, practicing his mercies
daily. There is no greater work appointed to you!
PETITIONER: Alleluia! Then to this great work of learning
to bear his likeness and his light, I commit my life.
INTERCESSOR: May he strengthen and encourage you,
and lead you gently in that good way.
Go in peace now to do his will.
TOGETHER: **Amen. To Christ be the glory. Amen.**

IF THE ONE SPEAKING THE PART OF THE INTERCESSOR ALSO NEEDS
TO HEAR THESE WORDS OF FREEDOM AND ENCOURAGEMENT
SPOKEN TO THEM, PETITIONER AND INTERCESSOR MAY NOW
SWITCH ROLES, AND WORK THROUGH THE LITURGY AGAIN.

A LITURGY FOR THE
Anniversary of a Loss

I have felt its approach in the back of my mind,
O Lord, like a burden tilting
toward me across the calendar.
I have felt its long approach,
and now it has arrived.

This is the day that marks the anniversary of my loss,
and waking to it, I must drink again from the stream of
a sorrow that cannot be fully remedied in this life.

O Christ, redeem this day.

I do not ask that these lingerings of grief be erased, but
that the fingers of your grace would work this memory
as a baker kneads a dough, till the leaven of
rising hope transforms it from within, into
a form holding now in that same sorrow the
surety of your presence, so that when I
look again at that loss, I see you
in the deepest gloom of it,
    weeping with me,
even as I hear you whispering that

this is not the end, but only
the still grey of the dawn
before the world begins.

And if that is so, then let that which broke me upon this day
in a past year, now be seen as the beginning
of my remaking into a Christ-follower more sympathetic,
more compassionate, and more conscious of my frailty and
of my daily dependence upon you; as one more invested
in the hope of the resurrection of the body
and the return of the King,
than ever I had been before.

Let this loss-hollowed day arrive in years to come
as the kindling of a fire in my bones, spurring me to
seek in this short life that which is eternal.
Let the past wound, and the memory of it, push me
to be present with you in ways that I was not before.

Do not waste my greatest sorrows, O God, but
use them to teach me to live in your presence—
fully alive to pain and joy and sorrow and hope—
in the places where my shattering
    and your shaping meet.

Amen.

A LITURGY FOR THE
Loss of a Living Thing

**BE AWARE OF THE EMOTIONS OF OTHER PARTICIPANTS,
PAUSING TO COMFORT ONE ANOTHER AS NECESSARY.**

LEADER: King of Creation,
Here was your good creature.

**A MOMENT OF SILENCE IS OBSERVED, THAT THOSE GATHERED
MIGHT CENTER THEIR THOUGHTS AND PREPARE THEIR HEARTS.**

Here was your good creature, O Lord,
pondered and called to life
by your own compassionate design.

**PEOPLE: Here was your good creature, and here were the
spaces and the days we shared, enjoying the glad company
and cheerful fellowship of a fellow creature.**

We made room in our lives,
    room in our home,
    room in our hearts,
to welcome your unique creation.
And we gave your good creature the name _____.

We were filled with a right and fond affection
for another living thing your hands had made,
delighting daily in its presence.

Now this season of our shared lives is ended by death.
Our hearts are unprepared for such loss,
    and we are deeply grieved.

Even so, Heavenly Father,
we are grateful for the life that was,
for the gift of a living thing so easily loved.

We are thankful for the many blessings
of knowing this creature, and for the lingering imprint
of such a cherished presence in our lives.
We are grateful for these good memories of sweeter times:

ONE OR MORE PARTICIPANTS MAY NOW RELATE
FOND MEMORIES OF THE CREATURE.

We are grateful, O God, for the happiness that was,
even as we mourn the sorrow that is,
even as we sit in the sadness of now empty spaces
in heart and home, empty spaces that echo our loss.
Now we say our goodbyes.

PARTICIPANTS MAY MEDITATE SILENTLY OR SPEAK ALOUD
IN TURN ANY FAREWELLS, AS THEY WISH.

O Lord, how long till all is made right?
How long till your wild grace restores all loss and
     upends every leaving?
**How long till these hurts are healed and these griefs
are eternally sealed and set aside by the finally completed
work of your redeeming love?**

We know if no sparrow falls beyond the ken of
your compassion, that you also, in this moment,
inhabit our sadness at this wounding, your weeping at the
world's brokenness somehow deeper than our own.

**Be near us, O God. Be near each of us who must
reckon with the sorrow of death and
the sting of separation, for what we feel in this loss
is nothing less than the groan of all creation.**

Our finite minds cannot trace the deeper mysteries of your
eternal mendings, but this we know with certainty:

**You are merciful and loving, gentle and compassionate,
caring tenderly for all that you have made.**

We know that the final working of your redemption will
be far-reaching, encompassing all things in heaven and
on earth, so that no good thing will be lost forever,

**so that even our sorrow at the loss of this beloved creature
will somehow, someday, be met and filled, and, in joy,
made forever complete.**

Comfort us in this meantime, O Lord, for
the ache of these days is real.

Amen.

A LITURGY FOR
Missing Someone

ALL STANDING AS ABLE, WITH EMPTY HANDS CUPPED.

LEADER: We willingly carry this ache.
PEOPLE: We carry it, O Father, to you.

PARTICIPANTS NOW SIT OR KNEEL IN A CIRCLE.

You created our hearts for unbroken fellowship.
Yet the constraints of time and place, and the
stuttering rhythms of life in a fallen world
dictate that all fellowships in these days
will at times be broken or incomplete.

And so we find ourselves in this season,
bearing the sorrow of our separation from _____.

SPEAK THE NAME OF THE ABSENT PERSON HERE.
FOR ADVENT OBSERVANCE, SPEAK THE NAME OF JESUS.

We acknowledge, O Lord, that it is
a right and a good thing to miss deeply
those whom we love but with whom
we cannot be physically present.
Grant us, therefore, courage to love well
even in this time of absence.

Grant us courage to shrink neither from
the aches nor from the joys that love brings,
for each, willingly received, will accomplish
the good works you have appointed them to do.
Therefore we praise you even for our sadness,
knowing that the sorrows we steward in this life
will in time be redeemed.

We praise you also knowing that these glad aches are a true
measure of the bonds you have wrought between our hearts.
**Now use our sorrows as tools in your hand, O Lord, shaping
our hearts into a truer imitation of the affections of Christ.**

Use even this sadness to carve out spaces in our souls
where still greater repositories of holy affection might
be held, unto the end that we might better love,
in times of absence and in times of presence alike.
We now entrust all to your keeping.
May our reunion be joyous, whether in this life
or in the life to come.
**How we look forward, O Lord, to the day when
all our fellowships will be restored, eternal and unbroken.
Amen.**

THE FOLLOWING SECTION MAY BE ADDED
DURING THE FIRST & SECOND WEEKS OF ADVENT.

O come, O come, Emmanuel!
Christ our King, how we long for your return.
O come, O come, Emmanuel!
Christ our Shepherd,   how we pine for your voice.
O come, O come, Emmanuel!
**Christ our older brother, how we miss you.
Make haste, O Lord. Return to us! Amen.**

THE FOLLOWING SECTION MAY BE ADDED
DURING THE THIRD AND FOURTH WEEKS OF ADVENT.

Remembering, O Christ, that you regarded our
helpless estate and came to dwell among us
as the promised fulfillment of all holy desires,
**we turn our hearts now
to remembrance of your works.**

SILENCE IS KEPT.

You came to us, O Lord, as a lantern in our darkness.
Now illumine our way.
You came to us as a song in the midst of our sorrow.
Now kindle our hope.
You came to us as a balm on the bed of our sufferings.
Now be our healing.
You came to us as a shelter amidst the violence of storms.
Now grant us peace.
You came to us as mercy in the place of our shame.
Now be our righteousness.
You came to us as a king upon the fields of our defeat.
Now be our salvation.
You came to us as a child in the midnight of our despair.
Now be our God.

Remembering these manifold joys and blessings
of your first advent, how our hearts long to
witness the glories of your promised return.
Come quickly, Lord Jesus!
O come, O come, Emmanuel.
Amen.

A LITURGY FOR
Leavings

LEADER: Even in our goodbyes there is a
blessing, for the sorrow of parting is a measure of
the depth of the bond we have come to share in Christ.
PEOPLE: **Thank you, O God,**
that we do not walk this road alone,
but that this journey toward eternity and toward your
heart has been, from the beginning, one that you
ordained we should undertake in the glad and
good company of our fellow pilgrims.

O Lord, make us ever mindful of one another
unto the end that we would labor in the
days to come as those who would tend and
encourage the stories of those around us by

prayer and friendship and thoughtfulness and
conversation, affirming and sharpening and amplifying
one another's good works, unto the end that your body
would be built up, and that your kingdom would be more
fully realized in this world.

**Thank you, O God, for the mercy and the beauty
incarnated in the words and acts of these
your people, extended one toward another.**
It is no accident that we were born in the same
epoch, and that our stories have twined in this time
    and in this place.

Let us therefore go forth and steward one another's stories.
Let us journey from here together, as vessels of that mercy
and as stewards of that wild and wondrous beauty that
flows from the heart and mind of our Creator.
**Grant, O Lord, that we might take our leave of one
another now, feeling a right joy for the blessings
of the hours we have shared, even as we feel
a bright and hopeful sorrow at their close.**

Friends and saints and fellow pilgrims, we part now in the
confidence that in our diverging paths we walk the
same road, fanning the same flame, and that in time
we will meet again in a fellowship forever unbroken.

By your Spirit, O Christ, make us faithful in the meanwhile,
as we go out to labor in the diverse fields
to which you have assigned us,
laboring unto that better meeting,
and unto that new-made world
that is yet promised and that has already begun.

O Spirit of God, be as present in our parting
as you were in our gathering.
Be present in our journeys.
Be present in our days to come.
Be present in our works and in our words and in our hearts.
Be present in the bonds of our community, Lord Christ.
Be ever at work among us and through us.

Amen.

A LITURGY FOR AN
Inconsolable Homesickness

Let me steward well, Lord Christ, this gift of homesickness—
this grieving for a childhood gone, this ache for distant family,
lost fellowship, past laughter, shared lives, and the sense
that I was somewhere I belonged.

It is a good, good thing to have a home.

But now that I have gone from it, let me steward well, O God,
this homesick gift, as I know my wish for what has been is
not some solitary ache, but is woven with a deeper longing for
what will one day be.

This yearning to return to what I knew is, even more than that,
a yearning for a place my eyes have yet to see.

So let me steward this sacred yearning well.
Homesickness is indeed a holy thing,
like the slow burning of an immortal beacon,
set ablaze to bid us onward.

The shape of that ache for another time and place is the
imprint of eternity within our souls. So let those sorrows
do their work in me, O God. Let them stir such yearnings
as would fix my journey forward toward
that place for which I've always pined.

O my soul, have there not always been signs?
O my soul, were we not born with hearts on fire?
Before we were old enough even to know
why songs and waves and starlight so stirred us,
had we not already tiptoed to the edge of that
vast sadness, bright and good, and felt ourselves
somehow stricken with a sickness unto life?

Hardly had we ventured from our yards,
when we felt ourselves so strangely far from
something—and somewhere that we despaired of
ever reaching—that we turned to hide the welling
of our eyes. We knew it, even then, as the opening of
a wound this world cannot repair—the first birthing
of that weight every soul must wake up to alone,
because it is the burden of that wild and lonely space that
only God in his eternity can fill.

And as we wait, this sacred, homesick sorrow works
in us to cultivate a faith that knows one day, he will.
That is the holy work of homesickness:
to teach our hearts how lonely
they have always been for God.

So let these sighs and tears, Lord Christ, prepare
me for that better gladness that will be mine.
Let all your children learn to grieve well in this life,
knowing we are not just being homesick;
we are letting sorrow carve the spaces in our souls,
that joy will one day fill.
O Holy Spirit, bless our grief,
and seal our hearts until that day.

Amen.

A LITURGY FOR THOSE FACING THE SLOW
Loss of Memory

When I no longer know the faces of my family,
　　Yet will you know me, O Lord.
When I can no longer remember my own name,
　　Yet will you remember me.

This will be my enduring hope,
until at last I wake from my long fog
into a bright morning of clarity
and see you face to face,
remembering again all that I had forgotten,
and knowing then even as I am known.

In light of this promise,
give me peace even now,
secure in the knowledge that what is obscured
from me is not truly lost, only tucked away and
waiting to be revealed fully in that eternal light.

O God, though all else be hid from me, all memory,
all knowledge, all understanding, do not hide your presence.
Be to me more present, more immediate, more abundant
in grace and peace, than ever I knew.

Though I know nothing else, still let me know you.
And if a morning dawns when I can no longer name you or
remember to call upon you, be more immediately present
to me then than my own confusion, than my own breath.
Be to me a peace and a light and an abiding sense that
I am loved and held and that all will be well.

Give grace and mercy also, O God,
to those who grieve my decline,
to those who love me, who must
suffer the heartache of such slow loss.
Bless their patient sacrifice on my behalf.
May their hope and their humor hold
and their hearts be strengthened beyond expectation.
Thank you for the years of health and love we
were given to share. May those memories and
your grace sustain them in sorrow.
Be near us now.

> O Father, in my weakness, be strong.
> O Jesus, in my loss, be found.
> O Spirit, in my absence, be present.

O God, in my forgetfulness, remember me, your child.

Amen.

A LITURGY FOR THE
Feeling of Infirmities

LEADER: We were not made for mortality but for immortality;
PEOPLE: **our souls are ever in their prime,**
and so the faltering of our physical bodies
    repeatedly takes us by surprise.

The aches, the frailties, the injuries, the
impositions of vexing disease and worsening
condition are unwelcome evidences of our
long exile from the Garden.

Even so, may the inescapable decline
of our bodies here not be wasted.
May it do its tutoring work, inclining
our hearts and souls ever more vigorously
toward your coming kingdom, O God.

While we rightly pray for healing and relief,
and sometimes receive the respite
of such blessings, give us also patience
for the enduring of whatever hardships
our journeys entail.

For what we endure here, in the deterioration
of bone and joint, blood and marrow,
muscle and ligament, vitality and mobility and clarity,
is but our own small share of the malady
common to a frayed creation
yet yearning for a promised restoration.

Give us humility therefore in our infirmities, to ask and
to receive, day by day, your mercies as our needs require.
Where our dependence on others increases, let us
receive their service as a grace rather than a shame.
Let us trace in the hands of our caregivers
the greater movement of your own hands,
for you ever meet us and uphold us in our weakness.
And in those moments when our bodies betray our trust,
work in us by our own hard experience a more active and
Christlike compassion for the sufferings of others.

Give us also a sense of humor to wink at our weaknesses now,
knowing that they are but the evidences of a perishable body
that will at your beckoning rise again imperishable, and that
the greater joke is the one played upon death.

By the inevitable dwindling of our strength,
may the mettle of our true hope at last be proved,
rising as the memory of a song stirring deep in the bones,

a martial melody of which our difficulties
are but the approaching drumbeat,
reminding us that this flesh and blood
are soon to be transformed, redeemed, remade.
The infirmities we incur today are but the expected
buffetings of a battle at which victorious end
our birthright will be forever reclaimed.

So may the decline of our bodies
incline our hearts and souls
ever more vigorously
toward your coming kingdom, O God.
Ever more vigorously.

Amen.

A LITURGY FOR THOSE
Fearing Failure

CHRISTIAN: **I come to you, O Christ,**
in dismay, fearing I might fail
in what is now before me.
FELLOW BELIEVER: Ah Christian,
if you would truly serve your Maker, in whatever capacity or

vocation, is it not necessary for your own good, and for the
good of the kingdom of God, that you would sometimes be
met with such fear and dismay?

**But how could such a besetting fear ever be for my good,
or for the good of God's eternal kingdom?**

Under the Spirit's tutelage, such fears might become
messengers of grace, revealing to you only
what was true all along:
>   in yourself you do not have the strength or the wisdom or
>   the ability to accomplish the task to which you are called.

Apart from the Spirit of God breathing life into
your incomplete and sin-tainted efforts,
apart from the Father blessing and multiplying your
inadequate offerings, apart from your Lord meeting you in
your stumbling attempts at faithfulness, no good work
will come to fruition, no achievement will endure,
no lasting benefit will come of your labors.

And so you must come repeatedly
to the end of trust in your own strength, child,
that you might avail yourself
again and again of his strength.

Then let my fears of failure drive me, O Lord,
to collapse here upon your strong shoulders, and
here to rest, reminded again that I and
all of your children are always utterly
dependent upon you to bring to completion,
in and through us, the good works which
you have prepared beforehand for us to do.
It is not my own work that is before me now, but yours!

Indeed Christian, take heart in this revelation!
The outcomes of your labors were never in your hands,
but in God's. You have but one task:
    to be faithful.

The success of your endeavors is not yours to judge.
He works in ways that you cannot comprehend.
And in his economy, there will be no waste.
Even what you judge as failure,
    God will tool to greater purpose.

If this is true,
    what greater end could he intend
    to work from my failings?

Who can discern? But consider now:
    Might your tender Father use even your failures

and weaknesses to make you more humble
and more sympathetic to the failures and failings of others,
thereby shaping your heart into a nearer likeness
of the heart of Christ?
If your greatest good is to bear in fuller measure
the image of your Lord, then might not his greatest
and most holy good to you come cloaked
in guise of defeat and dismay?

And if that is your Lord's sacred intention, then
who is to say how great a success even your failures
might be, when read aright at last in
the chronicles of eternity?
So relenquish now all vain attempts to parse
the mysteries of God's intent.
You cannot think his thoughts.
You cannot reckon his deep purposes.
It is enough to know that all he does
        is done in love for you.

**Amen. Use then, O Lord, even my failures, and
my fears of failing, to advance your purposes in
my heart and in your kingdom and in this world.
My confidence is only in you.**

Amen.

A LITURGY FOR THE

Death of a Dream

O Christ, in whom the final fulfillment
of all hope is held secure,

I bring to you now the weathered fragments of
my former dreams, the broken pieces of my expectations,
the rent patches of hopes worn thin, the shards of some
shattered image of life as I once thought it would be.

What I so wanted has not come to pass.
I invested my hopes in desires that returned only
sorrow and frustration. Those dreams, like glimmering
faerie feasts, could not sustain me,

    and in my head I know

     that you are sovereign even over this—

        over my tears, my confusion,

        and my disappointment.

But I still feel, in this moment, as if I have been abandoned,
as if you do not care that these hopes have collapsed to rubble.

And yet I know this is not so.
You are the sovereign of my sorrow.
You apprehend a wider sweep with wiser eyes than mine.

My history bears the fingerprints of grace.
You were always faithful, though I could not always
trace quick evidence of your presence in my pain,
yet did you remain at work, lurking in the wings,
sifting all my splinterings for bright embers that
might be breathed into more eternal dreams.

I have seen so oft in retrospect, how
you had not neglected me, but had,
with a master's care, flared my desire
like silver in a crucible to burn away
some lesser longing, and bring about
your better vision.

So let me remain tender now, to how
you would teach me. My disappointments
reveal so much about my own agenda for my life,
and the ways I quietly demand that it should play out:
        free of conflict, free of pain, free of want.

My dreams are all so small.

Your bigger purpose has always been
for my greatest good, that I would day-to-day be
fashioned into a more fit vessel
for the indwelling of your Spirit,

and molded into a more compassionate
emissary of your coming Kingdom.
And you, in love, will use all means to
shape my heart into those perfect forms.

So let this disappointment do its work.

My truest hopes have never failed, they have merely
been buried beneath the shoveled muck of disillusion,
or encased in a carapace of self-serving desire. It is only
false hopes that are brittle, shattering like shells of thin glass,
to reveal the diamond hardness of the unshakeable eternal
hopes within. So shake and shatter all that
would hinder my growth, O God.

Unmask all false hopes, that my one true hope might
shine out unclouded and undimmed. So let me be
tutored by this new disappointment. Let me listen
to its holy whisper, that I might release at last these lesser
dreams. That I might embrace the better dreams you
dream for me, and for your people, and for your kingdom,
and for your creation. Let me join myself to these,
investing all hope in the one hope that will never
come undone or betray those who place their trust in it.
Teach me to hope, O Lord,
        always and only in you.

You are the King of my collapse.
You answer not what I demand, but what I do not
even know to ask.

Now take this dream, this husk, this chaff of my desire, and
give it back reformed and remade according to your better
vision, or do not give it back at all. Here in the ruins of my
wrecked expectation, let me make this best confession:

Not my dreams, O Lord,
not my dreams,
but yours, be done.

Amen.

A LITURGY FOR THOSE WHO
Have Done Harm

My soul is chastened within me, O God.
Yet even in this crush of conviction
there flickers a spark of hope,
for you have told us you discipline those
whom you love.

I have harmed another, O Lord, and now
I have neither peace nor rest.
Yet I recognize in my own agitation the stirrings of
your Spirit who works in us, ever for our good.
I have run from your presence and from my conscience,
but I would run no more, O Lord.

I have hidden myself in shadows,
seeking to avoid your face,
even as did my father Adam and
my mother Eve in their first guilt.

I have drawn away from the sound of your voice,
fearful of what you might speak, fearful
of what obedience might require,
for I have sinned, O Father, and I am pained at this thought,
and shamed to bring my faults into the light.

Forgive me, most merciful Father,
for by sinning against one that you have placed
in my life for me to love and be merciful toward,
I have sinned against you.

I confess, O God, that I have broken faith, broken trust,
wounded another, and for this I repent.

HERE MAKE SPECIFIC CONFESSION EITHER TO GOD OR TO GOD IN
THE PRESENCE OF A MINISTER, PRIEST, OR FELLOW BELIEVER, BY
WHATEVER MEANS ARE MOST APPROPRIATE TO THE SITUATION.
ONCE CONFESSION HAS BEEN MADE, CONTINUE THE LITURGY.

Restorer of all things, redeem
the damage I have done.
Restore, remake, rekindle, rebuild.
Heal, comfort, and repair.
Knit together that which I have rent.

Use even the consequence of my sin to conform
my heart into a more fitting likeness of the heart of Christ.
Teach me true contrition and repentance that I would
fully face the consequences of my actions and choices,
asking forgiveness where necessary, making restitution
where possible, and caring more for the hurts of those
I have harmed than for the hope of my own
relief from the burdens of guilt.

Even as you used for good what Joseph's
brothers had intended for evil, O Lord,
so may the painful consequences
I have set in motion in the lives of others be
somehow redeemed in your providence.

Give me patience. Let me not respond in
shame or frustration when one
whom I have offended is not easily
able to forgive. When I am reminded again
of the depth of hurt I have caused,
may I be willing to sit again in my contrition,
understanding that healing can be a long work,
and that I have neither right nor means to
force the healing of the heart of another.

O God, be merciful.
Do not add to my sin
the weight of having placed
upon another a burden of unforgiveness
that will eat at their soul like a cancer.

For their sake, O Lord, grant them the grace
of true forgiveness and the freedom
that would follow from it.
Let them rise to continue their journey
toward you unhindered,
        even if the personal consequence of my own sin
        is that I can no longer walk closely beside them.

And let me rise from this conviction and confession
wiser in my faith, more intentional in my love for others,

less likely to choose the dried husk of selfishness
when next tempted toward sin.

I know that my tendency is to hide
my ill desires and temptations,
allowing them to give birth to sinful action.
Therefore bless me with the fellowship
of a true community, bonded by holy love,
that walks together in transparency,
conviction, and generosity of spirit,
wherein I might daily avail myself
of such means of grace
that I would live more accountable,
and less likely to harm again.

Forgive me, O Lord, lest I despair.
Restore me, lest I be forever lost.
For your pardon alone is sufficient to my peace;
and your death to my resurrection.
Embrace me again to life and to right standing with you,
O God, and to the fellowship of love and compassion
    that is your church.

I am always, every moment, in need of you.

Amen.

A LITURGY FOR THOSE WHO
Weep Without Knowing Why

There is so much lost in this world, O Lord,
so much that aches and groans and shivers
for want of redemption, so much that
seems dislocated, upended, desecrated,
unhinged—even in our own hearts.

Even in our own hearts
we bear the mark of all that is broken.
What is best in this world has been bashed
and battered and trodden down.
What was meant to be the substance has
become the brittle shell, haunted by the
ghosts of a glory so long crumbled that only
its rubble is remembered now.

Is it any wonder we should weep sometimes,
without knowing why? It might be anything.
And then again, it might be everything.

For we feel this.
We who are your children feel this empty space where
some lost thing should have rested in its perfection,

and we pine for those nameless glories, and we pine
for all the wasted stories in our world, and we pine for
these present wounds. We pine for our children and for their
children too, knowing each will have to prove how this
universal pain is also personal. We pine for all children born
into these days of desolation—whose regal robes were
torn to tatters before they were even swaddled in them.

O Lord, how can we not weep,
when waking each day in this vale of tears?
How can we not feel those pangs, when we,
wounded by others, so soon learn to wound as well,
and in the end wound even ourselves?
We grieve what we cannot heal and
we grieve our half-belief, having made
uneasy peace with disillusion, aligning
ourselves with a self-protective lie
that would have us kill our best hopes just
to keep our disappointments half-confined.

We feel ourselves wounded by what is wretched,
foul, and fell, but we are sometimes wounded by the
beauty as well, for when it whispers, it whispers of
the world that might have been our birthright, now banished,
now withdrawn, as unreachable to our wounded hearts as
ancient seas receding down some endless dark.

We weep, O Lord, for those things that, though
nameless, are still lost. We weep for the cost of our
rebellions, for the mocking and hollowing of holy things,
for the inward curve of our souls, for the evidences of death
outworked in every field and tree and blade of grass,
crept up in every creature, alert in every longing,
infecting all fabrics of life.

We weep for the leers our daughters will endure, as if
to be made in reflection of your beauty were a fault for
which they must pay. We weep for our sons, sabotaged by profi-
teers who seek to warp their dreams before they even
come of age. We weep for all the twisted alchemies of
our times that would turn what might have been gold into
crowns of cheap tin and then toss them into refuse bins
as if love could ever be a castoff thing
one might simply be done with.

We weep for the wretched expressions of all
things that were first built of goodness and glory
but are now their own shadow twins.
We have wept so often.
And we will weep again.

And yet, there is somewhere in our tears
a hope still kept.

We feel it in this darkness,
like a tiny flame,
when we are told

Jesus also wept.

You wept.

So moved by the pain of this crushed creation, you, O Lord,
heaved with the grief of it, drinking the anguish like
water and sweating it out of your skin like blood.

Is it possible that you—in your sadness over Lazarus,
in your grieving for Jerusalem, in your sorrow in the garden—
is it possible that you have sanctified our weeping too?

For the grief of God is no small thing,
and the weeping of God is not without effect.
The tears of Jesus preceded a resurrection of the dead.

O Spirit of God, is it then possible that
our tears might also be a kind of intercession?

That we, your children, in our groaning
with the sadness of creation, could
be joining in some burdened work

of coming restoration? Is it possible that when
we weep and don't know why, it is because
the curse has ranged so far, so wide? That
we weep at that which breaks your heart, because
it has also broken ours—sometimes so deeply that
we cannot explain our weeping,
even to ourselves?

If that is true,
then let such weeping be received, O Lord,
as an intercession newly forged of holy sorrow.
Then let our tears anoint these broken things,
and let our grief be as their consecration—
a preparation for their promised redemption,
our sorrow sealing them for that day when
you will take the ache of all creation,
and turn it inside-out,
like the shedding of
an old gardener's glove.

O Lord, if it please you,
when your children weep and don't know why,
      yet use our tears
      to baptize what you love.

Amen.

LITURGIES OF
The Moment

MOMENTARY LITURGIES FOR PRACTICING THE
Presence of God

SMALL LITURGIES DESIGNED TO BE PRAYED SILENTLY OR SPOKEN ALOUD, TO HELP DIRECT THE HEART TOWARD THE HEART'S CREATOR.

UPON SEEING A BEAUTIFUL PERSON

Lord, I praise you for divine beauty
reflected in the form of this person.
Now train my heart so that my response to their beauty
would not be twisted downward into envy or desire,
but would instead be directed upward in worship of you,
their Creator—as was your intention for all such beauty
before the breaking of the world.

UPON TASTING A PLEASURABLE FOOD

For the infinite variety of your creative expression,
I praise you, O God. You have made even the necessary act
of eating a nurturing comfort and a perpetual delight.

UPON EXPERIENCING CHEERING LAUGHTER

I praise you, O God, for these inexplicable gifts of mirth
and merriment and laughter, delighting in such foretaste
of the wellsprings of eternal joy that ever bubble and flow
within your glad Trinity.

UPON RANDOMLY THINKING OF ANOTHER PERSON

God, as I hold _____ a moment in my thoughts,
I ask that you would hold them eternally in yours,
remaining ever at work in their heart and life, even now
directing their paths toward your good ends.

UPON BEING MOVED BY A SONG OR A PIECE OF MUSIC

O Lord, let such melodies penetrate my heart's defenses,
gently revealing old wounds unto their eventual healings,
gently stirring eternal longings unto the restoration of hope.

 or

Tune my heart, my mind, my life,
 to voice your melodies, O God.

UPON HEARING BIRDSONG

You draw praise from the frailest of things.
 So also draw praise from me.

UPON SIGHTING A FLOWER IN BLOOM

O Lord who so lavishly adorns the fields,
 how radiant must your eternal glories be!

UPON AN UNEXPECTED SIGHTING OF WILDLIFE

O Christ who sustains all wild creatures,
 care also for me, thy child.

UPON OBSERVING A TREE SWAYING IN WIND
O Spirit of God who moves in mystery unseen,
   so move now in my heart.

UPON FEELING THE PLEASANCE OF A WARM SHOWER
Thank you, O Lord, for gifts of water and warmth, and for
the cleansing and comfort you offer both body and soul.

A LITURGY FOR
The Sound of Sirens

The wail of sirens is the anthem of our brokenness,
reminding us that fear and tragedy, pain and crime
yet plague a creation groaning for its redemption.

Therefore attend those now in crisis, O Lord,
remaining ever merciful and mindful of their frailties.
May their first cry be to you, and may such cries be met
by your presence and your peace.

Grant good judgment to those who minister aid and
protection, and comfort all who endure trauma or loss.
Use even these parts of our stories which are accompanied
by sirens, O Lord, to press us closer to your heart.

A LITURGY FOR A
Fleeting Irritation

I bring to you Lord, my momentary irritation,
that you might reveal the buried seed of it—not
in the words or actions of another person, but
in the withered and hypocritical expectations
of my own small heart. Uproot from this
impoverished soil all arrogance and insecurity that
would prompt me to dismiss or disdain others,
judging them with a less generous measure than
I reckon when judging myself.
Prune away the tangled growth
of my own unjustified irritations, Jesus,
and graft to my heart instead your humility,

>   your compassion,

>   your patience,

>   your kindness,

that I might bear good fruit in keeping
with your grace.

Amen.

A LITURGY FOR
Moments of Emergency

LEADER: O God our Rock,
PEOPLE: **hold us in this chaos.**

O Christ our King,
calm us in this storm.

O Holy Spirit,
Intercede for us.

Be merciful, most merciful God!

O God our Rock,
hold us in the chaos of this hard hour.

O Christ our King,
calm us in the storm of our distress.

O Holy Spirit,
Intervene and intercede.

We need you now, most merciful God!

A LITURGY FOR A
Moment of Frustration at a Child

Let me not react in this moment, O Lord,
in the blindness of my own emotion.

Rather give me—
    a fellow sinner—
wisdom to respond with a grace
that would shepherd my child's heart
toward your mercies,
    so equipping them
    for the hard labors
    of their own pilgrimage.

A LITURGY FOR EXPERIENCING
Road Rage

If my heart were more content in you, O Lord,
I would be less inclined to rage at others.
Let me gauge by the knot in my gut,
the poverty of my own understanding
of the grace that I have received
from a God who, loving me,

    chose rather to receive wounds
      than to give them.
Take from me my self-righteousness,
and my ego-driven demands for respect.
Overthrow the tyranny of my anger, O Lord,
and in its place establish a better vision
    of your throne,
    your kingdom,
    and your peace.

Amen.

A LITURGY FOR
Waiting in Line

As my life is lived in anticipation
of the redemption of all things,
so let my slow movement in this line
be to my own heart
a living parable and a teachable moment.
Do not waste even my petty irritations, O Lord.
Use them to expose my sin and selfishness
    and to reshape my vision
    and my desire into better, holier things.

Decrease my unrighteous impatience,
directed at circumstances and people.
Increase instead my righteous longing
for the moment of your return,
when all creation will be liberated
from every futility in which it now languishes.

Be present in my waiting, O Lord,
that I might also be present in it
as a Christ-bearer to those before
    and behind me,
        who also wait.

As I am a vessel,
let me not be like a sodden paper cup
full of steaming frustration, carelessly
sloshing unpleasantness on those around me.
Rather let me be like a communion chalice,
reflecting the silvered beauty of your light,
brimming with an offered grace.

Amen.

LITURGIES OF
Table
Blessings

A LITURGY FOR
Sunday's Table Blessing

LEADER: O God and Father of All,

PEOPLE: **We are gathered at this table**
in grateful fellowship to share
the blessing of this meal at the
christening of this new week.

We lift to you here our hearts and prayers.

For grace and provision in the coming week,
we look to you.
For the lifegiving gifts of your word and your truth,
we are thankful.
For the joys of life shared with family and friends,
we praise you.

For the grace to live in grateful humility,
we look to you.
For the many small blessings and beauties that surround us,
we are thankful.
For the displays of your majesty and power in our world,
we praise you.

For the promise of your constant presence,
giving hope and comfort and strength
and joy in the various moments
and labors of the week to come,
we bless your holy name.

May the rhythms of our petitions
and thanksgivings
become, in time,
like the steady drumbeat
in a long and unending song
of your faithfulness, O God.

Amen.

AS WE SHARE THIS SUNDAY MEAL, WE SHARE ALOUD OUR HOPES, OUR
PLANS, OUR CONCERNS AND OUR PRAYERS FOR THE WEEK TO COME.

A LITURGY FOR
Monday's Table Blessing

LEADER: O God our rock,
PEOPLE: **We thank you that you did not leave us
rudderless and tossed by storms in this life,**

but have graciously given us,
in your word, and in the witness of
the life and words of your son,
a true mooring for our own lives,
a true anchor for our souls.

**Your words are life to us,
Lord Christ.**

Even as we hunger for the tastes
and textures and aromas of
this meal now graciously spread before us,
**we pray you would also daily increase
our deep hunger for your words and your truth,**
that our own words
and choices
and actions
this week would be shaped
by your gracious revelation.

Feed us, O Bread of Life.

Amen.

AS WE SHARE THIS MEAL, WE SPEAK OF TRUTHS WE ARE
LEARNING, AND QUESTIONS WE ARE CONSIDERING.

A LITURGY FOR
Tuesday's Table Blessing

LEADER: Christ our closest companion,
PEOPLE: **For the consolations of friendship and fellowship,**
for the blessings of family and of the family of God,
for the assurance that we do not walk this week's road alone,
but are gathered into community, making good pilgrimage
together through this life and towards the eternal city,
we thank you.

For the assurance that you go before us
and also walk beside us, Lord Christ,
we thank you all the more.

For your tender care displayed
in the food and friends now before us,
we offer you our praise.

How blessed we are to be called your children.
How blessed to be adopted into your family.
Blessed be your name, O God, Father, Son, and Holy Spirit.

Amen.

WE SHARE THIS TUESDAY MEAL AS PILGRIMS PAUSING IN THEIR
TRAVELS TO TELL ONE ANOTHER TALES OF THEIR RECENT JOURNEYS.

A LITURGY FOR
Wednesday's Table Blessing

LEADER: O Christ who emptied himself for us,
Give us today the gift of humility
PEOPLE: **so that we would realize a true
thankfulness for things we too often
take for granted.**

We would remember and thank you today
for these most precious gifts:
    for life and
    for breath,
    for shelter,
    for this meal and all meals, and
    for a span of days
in which to live and choose what use
we would make of our time.

**Give us grace to make wise investment
of the days you have given us this week,
that by our thoughts and words and actions
we might love you well.**

As we pause at this cresting of the week,
guide us, O Spirit of God,
in a brief and sober reflection
on our daily stewardships and habits.
**Guide us, O God. Search now
our willing hearts.**

A SHORT, PRAYERFUL SILENCE IS KEPT.

Now, Holy Spirit, who for love of your children
offers both conviction and comfort, give
encouragement and tender correction to
each as needed,
**unto the end that our life and breath
and span of days would not be squandered,
but would be well-spent in your service.**

Amen.

AS WE SHARE THIS WEDNESDAY MEAL, WE TAKE TIME TO FIND OUT
HOW EACH IS FARING IN THE MID-WEEK CROSSING.

A LITURGY FOR
Thursday's Table Blessing

LEADER: O King of Joys Eternal,
today we praise you for small wonders;
PEOPLE: **in them we see your delight.**

For birds that trill and warble their worship,
for the verdant witness of windblown leaves,
and of starlight sparkling, and of sunlit streams,
and of blooming flowers,

We praise you, O King.
Your joy is everywhere manifest,
     even in the smallest things.

We praise you, O King,
for soft beds and blankets,
for stories and songs,
for kisses and kindnesses.
Your tenderness is displayed
in all things nurturing.

Your mercy is manifest in the details of this world, O Lord.
Your grace is worked into every corner of creation,

Your care is evident in the fabric
of all created things,
even in the pleasurable and
nourishing properties of this meal.
For this food and for all small wonders,
we give you thanks and we
give you praise, O God.

Amen.

AS WE SHARE THIS THURSDAY MEAL, WE CULTIVATE OUR
THANKFULNESS FOR THE SMALL WONDERS OF THE WEEK BY
TELLING OF SOMETHING WE HAVE PAUSED TO APPRECIATE.

A LITURGY FOR
Friday's Table Blessing

LEADER: O God of power and strength,
PEOPLE: **Today we offer praise for things**
larger and mightier than ourselves:
    for towering cloud columns,
    for lightning flash
    and thunder crack,
    for rugged rise of mountain

and seething swell of oceans in storm,
for rushing wind
and spiring tree,
for love greater than we can comprehend.
For these we give you thanks,
for they remind us that we are small beside
you, our Maker, and that we are the children
of a mighty God and Father.

We give you thanks for all things magnificent,
mighty, massive, monumental, for great creatures
and colossal planets and all things that set us
in awe of what is vaster than ourselves.
These things render us good service, O Lord,
for the wonder they inspire is a window directing
our eyes and our thoughts to you, who are vaster
and more infinite and awesome, who are fiercer
in your love and mightier in your strength
and more holy in your righteousness
than all created things.

We, your children, are small before you,
but we are greatly loved.

And so we bow now our heads in thanks,
gratefully receiving from your great hand

**the provision of this meal,
and the still greater provisions
of your mercy, your compassion,
your grace, your love.**

Amen.

AS WE SHARE THIS MEAL, WE CONSIDER TOGETHER SOME OF THE
MIGHTY WORKS OF GOD, DISPLAYED IN THE BOOK OF SCRIPTURE
AND IN THE BOOK OF NATURE, AND IN OUR OWN LIVES.

A LITURGY FOR
Saturday's Table Blessing

LEADER: Christ our Captain, Christ our King,
for your constant presence with us
in the week now passed,
PEOPLE: **we thank you, O Lord.**

For your faithful provision in those days,
we bless your name.
For the sustenance and shelter and good
company that were ours,

we give you praise.
In the bounty that graces our table
even this hour, at the closing of this week,
we see new evidence of your
shepherding love.

We will not live this week again.
Therefore may our hearts,
under the perfect tutelage of your Spirit,
now glean wisdom
from the memory of
our passage through
the moments and
emotions of those days.

We pray your purposes in our lives
would be accomplished, O God,
that in the new week to come
we would somehow be changed
by the work of your Spirit,
that you would be active in us,
ever sanctifying our desires
and Christ-shaping our hearts.

We give you thanks, O Lord,
    for the week that was,

and for the day that is,

and for the morrow that is yet to come,

knowing that

as you have been faithful

so are you faithful,

and so will you be faithful

forever more.

Amen.

AS WE SHARE THIS MEAL, WE TELL STORIES OF GOD'S FAITHFULNESS
IN THE WEEK THAT HAS BEEN, ALSO OF MOMENTS WE HAVE ENJOYED
OR THAT WERE SIGNIFICANT TO US.

Benediction

A LITURGY OF
Praise to the King of Creation

LEADER: Our thoughts of you,
O Lord, have been too small, too few—
for seldom have we considered
how specific is the exercising of your authority,
extending as it does into the myriad particulars of creation.

PEOPLE: **There is no quarter over which you are not king.**

And as creation hurtles toward its liberation and
redemption, the full implications of your deep Lordship
are yet to be revealed in countless facets unconsidered:

> **Christ, you are the Snow King.**
> **You are the Maker of All Weathers.**
> **You are The King of Sunlight and Storms,**
> **The King of Grey Skies and Rain.**
> **You are The Rain King,**
> **The Sun King,**
> **the Hurricane King.**
> **You are the King of Autumn**
> **and King of Spring.**

And our thoughts of you,
O Lord, have been too small, too few.

The old and impotent gods
our ancestors once believed in were,
at their best,
but imperfect pictures of you, whose strength
and goodness and creative majesty
and wonderful mystery and love exceed those
old rumors as sunlight exceeds the tiny dimness
of stars reflected in a dark and wavering pool.

The fairy tales crafted by our old cultures
hinted at you, though they knew it not.
Yet their perfect princes and blessed ends were
yearnings for all that has found fulfillment in you.

> **You are the Lord of the Harvest.**
> **The Grain King,**
> **The Wine King,**
> **The God of Plenty,**
> **The God of Hearth and Home.**
> **You are The Hill King,**
> **The Wildflower King,**
> **King of the Great Bears,**
> **King of Canyons.**

You are The Monarch of Meadows,
The Lord of the Lava Fields,
Ruler of the Desert Wastes,
The Polar King,
The Rainbow King,
The King of the Southern Cross,
and The King of the Northern Lights.

You are the King of the Rabbits,
and The Lord of Tall Trees.
You are the God of Youth
and the God of Age.
You are The Acorn King,
The River God,
The Swamp King,
King of Glades,
King of Dells,
Ruler of All Hummingbirds.

You are The Horse Lord,
The Crag King,
Lord of the Bees,
King of the Walruses,
Commander of Rhinos,
Lord of the Lightning Bugs,

Cave Lord,
Mountain King,
Ruler of the Grassy Plains,
God of the Valleys.

You are The Captain of the Clouds,
The Wolf King,
The King of the Cockatoos.

And our thoughts of you,
O Lord, have been too small, too few.

For your claim over creation is vast. You are
The Lord of Antarctica,
the King of California,
the King of the Scottish Hills,
and the King of the Nile.

You are the weaver of
the unseen fabrics of the world.
You are Lord of the Atoms,
The Ruler of Electrons,
The Lord of Gravity,
and The King of Quarks.

Your dominion enfolds the earth and rises
beyond it to the furthest extremes of the stars.

    You are Lord of the Vast Empty Spaces.
    You are The King of the Constellations,
    The Black Hole King,
    Lord of Novas Exploding,
    Lord of Speeding Light,
    High King of Galaxies,
    King of Orion,
    King of the Moon.

**And still, even still,
our thoughts of you
have been too small,
too few.**

    You are the God of Justice,
    The God of Wisdom,
    The God of Mercy,
    The God of Redemption.

    You are The Lord of Love.

All of this is true.
But our thoughts of you are still too few,
for our minds are too small

to conceive of them all,
let alone to contain them.

**You were before all things,
you created all things, and
in you all things are held together.
There is no corner of creation
you will fail to redeem.**

You are Lord of Lords,
and King of Kings,
**O Jesus Christ,
our King of Everything.**

Amen.

Dying
& Grieving

AN EXCERPT FROM A NEW
EVERY MOMENT HOLY
COLLECTION FOR USE
DURING SEASONS OF
DYING & GRIEVING
—COMING IN 2020

A LITURGY FOR
Dying Well

O Lord Who Ordained
the Measure of My Days Before Time
and Creation Began, let me finish
well this brief race I have run.

In this season of close-reckoning
my own mortality, may I meet you
in each moment of sadness or regret;
when dwelling in the long shadows
cast by fear, let me yet take comfort
in this bright thought:

That even as I rightly lament all I stand
to lose by dying—the longed for days I
will not live to share with those I love,
the dreams I will at last release
unrealized—that even so, O Lord, you in
your wisdom and mercy did gift me more
hours than were necessary for my heart to
warm to your love, for my pride to crumble
beneath the weight of your mercies, for
my mind to be convinced that I am your

dearly-loved child, and for my hopes to grow
firm-anchored in the promise of a new creation
and of my own coming resurrection.

In light of these future glories,
let me learn to trust you more fully
with my present sorrows,
that I might lean upon you
in my remaining steps, Great Shepherd,
more surely even than I leaned upon you
in seasons past. Be in these days
the comfort in my pain, the peace
that quiets my fear, the consolation that
speaks a better word than any grief or regret.

Though some will write off
the remainder of my days as of no value,
I know that you will not, else you would never
have ordained that I should live them.
Trusting your providence, I would not now
dismiss them either.

For it is by your pleasure that I am still
alive in this holy moment; that I still wake
to love, hope, pray, feel, dream, grieve, and
do the next thing and the next thing that
must be done, so long as my strength allows.

Nothing true and eternal has changed simply
because I received an unwelcome diagnosis. We
have always been moving—even from our births—
toward that approaching moment when life would
be swallowed up in immortality.

So much as it is an act of will then, I would
offer to you, moment-by-moment, O God,
this final pilgrimage
and every blessing and hardship
that will attend it.

Though my body declines and I find myself
beset by new pains, discomforts, and limitations,
I am yet your servant as truly as ever, still
your child, still a vessel of your indwelling
Spirit, still a recipient and a conduit of your grace.

Redeem then these precious remaining days.
And make of me what you will,
even now, in this season of my dying.
Shape me yet in whatever time is left.
For this was always my best vocation:
to grow into a truer and truer
image-bearer of my God, learning to
know you, trust you, love you more.

My worth to you was never the measure
of what I could do or accomplish by my own hand.
All along, you passionately loved me as your child,
delighting to lead me by your Spirit into closer
and more constant communion with yourself.

And so my life will be no less significant
in the moment I draw my last breath
than it was in the moment I drew my first.
For each of those breaths—
and all between—
are set within the span
you ordained for me to live and move and
breathe in this body, in this world. All
moments are equally fraught with your love,
your wonder, your holiness, your purpose,
however clouded and inscrutable
such mystery might sometimes seem
amidst the hurts and harms of a broken world.

So use even these days of hard experience,
O Spirit of God, to further your sanctifying
work in me. Convince me ever more firmly of
my great need, and of your great grace,
of my own sin and weakness,

and of your strength and forgiveness;
of my own utter helplessness,
and of your merciful provision.

I entrust all things to you, Jesus.

For you are the Captain
of my passage through this storm.
You are the King
who leads me home from lonely exile.
You are the Lover
who embraces me in the midst of my grief.
You are the Redeemer
of all lost and broken things
now yearning to be made new.

Your mercies are everlasting and your promises are true.

You are the very author of life, and
the conqueror of death, who has promised
to remake this world, this sky, these gardens
and cities and stars, and also, yes, my own
failing flesh, raising it new and imperishable.

So seal my heart unto that day, O Christ.
So inhabit these holy spaces,

these hardships and sorrows,
this precious hope of glory.
So cradle me in my present frailties.
So commune with me in my grief.
So shepherd my passing.

So command my resurrection.

Amen.

DOUGLAS KAINE MCKELVEY grew up in East Texas and moved to Nashville in 1991. In the decades since, he has worked as an author, song lyricist, scriptwriter, and video director. He and his wife Lise have three grown daughters and two sons-in-law.

SOME OF HIS OTHER BOOKS INCLUDE:
The Angel Knew Papa and the Dog (illustrated by Zach Franzen), *Stories We Shared: A Family Book Journal* (with Jamin Still), *The Wishes of the Fish King* (illustrated by Jamin Still), *Locust Pocus* (illustrated by Richard Egielski), *A Child's Christmas at St. Nicholas Circle* (art by Thomas Kinkade), and "The Places Beyond the Maps" in the *Wingfeather Tales*

NED BUSTARD is a graphic designer, author, illustrator, and printmaker for World's End Images, the creative director for Square Halo Books, Inc., and curator of the Square Halo Gallery. He and his wife Leslie have three grown daughters.

SOME OF HIS OTHER BOOKS INCLUDE:
It Was Good: Making Art to the Glory of God, History of Art: Creation to Contemporary, Bible History ABC's, Bigger on the Inside: Christianity and Doctor Who, Revealed: A Storybook Bible for Grown-Ups, and the Rabbit Room's edition of George MacDonald's *The Light Princess.*

The Rabbit Room (named for the back room of the pub
where the Inklings —J. R. R. Tolkien, C. S. Lewis,
Charles Williams, and others—shared their stories)
fosters Christ-centered community and
spiritual formation through art, music, and story.
For more information visit:

RABBITROOM.COM